The experiences of an or~~di~~   'odge
which came to initia~~   ~~   ar.
             &

Design and illustrations by Lawrie Morrisson

Music by Eric Stuckey

W. Bro. Ed Fehler, the Master who started our adventure, on our 75th anniversary with W. Bro. Ken Birnie, then Assistant Provincial Grand Master and a source of constant support.

Proceeds accruing to the author and designer will be donated to the Benevolent Fund of St Laurence Lodge, No. 5511.

The scripts and a recording of the music can be downloaded at http://stlaurencelodge.org.uk/publications/entertainments/.

Text © David John West; cover design and photographs © Lawrie Morrisson. Other illustrations are acknowledged at the end of the book. First published in the United Kingdom in 2014.

ISBN: 978-0-9928572-0-2

> The right of Dr David John West to be identified as the author of this work has been asserted in accordance with sections 77 and 78 of the Copyright Designs and Patents Act 1988. All rights reserved. No part of this publication may be reproduced, stored in a retrieval system, or transmitted in any form or by any means, electronic, mechanical, photocopying, recording or otherwise, without prior permission from the copyright holder. Notwithstanding the above, permission is granted to any regular Masonic lodge to perform within that lodge and as part of a lodge meeting any of the plays, entertainments or lectures contained in this volume for as long as the copyright and the name and number of the St Laurence Lodge, No. 5511 is acknowledged in any advertisement or notice for and of such performance.

Published by Hamilton House Publishing Ltd, Rochester, Kent.

Printed by Graphy Cems, Navarra, Spain.

Distributed by Lewis Masonic, www.lewismasonic.com.

Lewis Masonic

Riverdene Business Park, Molesey Road, Hersham, Surrey KT12 4RG.

The author, the designer and two ever willing accomplices;
(l to r) Ken, Lawrie, David and Andrew.

ಌ ಌ ಌ

This book is dedicated to the members of St Laurence Lodge, No. 5511, who seem ever ready to participate in whatever scheme we dream up.

ಌ ಌ ಌ

I am grateful to many people for their assistance in writing this book but the opinions expressed remain my own. This book does not represent the opinions of the United Grand Lodge of England, the Masonic Province of Essex, St Laurence Lodge No. 5511 nor any of my brethren. I would like to state quite firmly that it has no official status whatsoever and that all errors are mine. (Though personally, I'd blame Lawrie!)

ಌ ಌ ಌ

Though this be madness, yet there is method in't. (Hamlet Act 2 Sc 2)

Insanity is repeating the same mistakes and expecting different results.
(Narcotics Anonymous)

Brethren meeting nine candidates — a happy gathering at a bowling alley.

Contents

Foreword — 1
W. Bro. John Helliar, Past Senior Grand Deacon United Grand Lodge of England

Feelin' good is easy — 3
There are many men anxious to become members of our institution. They simply have not found a friendly way in.

Easy changes to start with — 5
Improving talks in lodge, improving the festive board, table planning, public speaking, nerves, preparation, getting started, hooks and themes, using jokes, bringing the speech to an end, using a quiz at the festive board.

Not lectures but Lectures — 20
The ritual of early lodge meetings, the Lectures as the real thing, simple uses, choosing sections, costume & props, using older versions.

Catechism! — 31
An entertainment demonstrating the beauty of the Lectures.

The law of paradoxical intent — 47
Doing the same old, same old, won't help.

Charge! — 51
An entertainment about the ancient charges and the Old Charges, showing the moral basis of our order unchanged since 1390.

Attacks on Freemasonry — 65
The ravers from 1698 to Stephen Knight.

Attack! — 71
An entertainment featuring early attacks on the Craft, Stephen Knight, Jack the Ripper, the Seddon case — with an explanation.

Exposure! — 85
An entertainment using 18th century exposures of the ritual, featuring Prichard's 'Masonry Dissected' and exposing a dreadful cover up.

The truth about the words — 107
Shock! Horror! The established theory is wrong.

A White Table — 112
The complete 'how-to' with a full script and a discussion of openness.

Success — 141
The design and use of websites, a caution, being interesting, contacts and how to manage them, getting to know candidates, mentoring recruits.

Triple! — 150
How to initiate three candidates at one meeting in a dramatic but personal way.

Music for *Exposure!* — 176
The score; for a download of the recorded music go to
http://stlaurencelodge.org.uk/publications/entertainments/

Foreword

W. Bro. John Helliar

Past Senior Grand Deacon of the United Grand Lodge of England, Past Assistant Provincial Grand Master of the Province of Essex, Provincial Prior of the Knights Templar in Essex.

I was delighted to accept the invitation to provide a foreword to this book, *Things to do when you have nothing to do*. Freemasonry has faced many challenges since the formation of the first Grand Lodge in 1717 and today many lodges find themselves short of candidates, without ritual to perform. We have faced many challenges in our history with the same two options; to sit back and complain or make the changes demanded of us. W. Bro. David West's book shows us a way to rise to the challenges we face today.

It is not a theoretical account but one based on the real life experience of St Laurence Lodge No. 5511, of which I have been an honorary member since my retirement from the Assistant Provincial Grand Mastership of Essex. I can assure you that everything in this book works, because I have seen it working.

This book will not only give you interesting and enjoyable work to do, it will also lead you towards candidates. It is subtitled *How to find those candidates who have been looking for you all this time* and this is no empty boast. St Laurence genuinely initiates three to four candidates a year and genuinely does have a growing waiting list. It really does take most of its second and third degrees out to other lodges and it does run an extra meeting each year when a guest team carries out an initiation. Indeed, I have led such a guest team myself (*see photo*).

During my time as Assistant Provincial Grand Master, I encountered successful and less successful lodges. I often felt that there was a cycle in the fortunes of lodges: without a candidate for three or four years, a lodge would suddenly find a rich vein that brought new brethren into Freemasonry. Nevertheless, some lodges maintain a constant stream of candidates while yet others are forced surrender their warrants when no new brethren appear to replace the ageing members. I have also found that there is no panacea, that what works in one lodge does not do so in another.

However, I have always been impressed — and even more so in the last four or five years — with the brethren of St Laurence Lodge and the standards they seek and maintain. I first visited the lodge as a young mason over thirty years ago and have seen it grow, not without some difficult times, into the vibrant, exciting and forward thinking lodge it has now become.

Without doubt, in David West and Lawrie Morrisson, they have two of the most far sighted and innovative Freemasons in Essex, ably assisted as they are by other enthusiastic brethren. In fact the whole lodge embraces new ideas to attract the right calibre of candidates and uses all the tools of modern technology to spread the message of Freemasonry. Their website, for example, is the envy of the many who seek to follow in the footsteps of St Laurence Lodge No. 5511 and replicate its success.

I am not saying it is easy — but I am saying it works.

ರು ರು ರು

Raffling a cake from the 'St Laurence Cakers' — brethren who like to bake.

Feelin' good is easy

Freedom's just another word for nothin' left to lose.
Nothin' ain't worth nothin' but it's free.
Feeling good was easy Lord, when Bobby sang the blues.
Feeling good was good enough for me,
Good enough for me and Bobby McGee.

Kris Kristofferson and Fred Foster. First recorded by Roger Miller.

The absence of ritual for a meeting often brings on the blues. With no work to do, the lodge is free to do whatever it wants — but all too often this means a desperate search to find someone, anyone, willing to entertain the brethren. *Freedom's just another word for nothin' left to lose*, perhaps. When *All we had at our last meeting was a talk*, the brethren feel bad and the fact is that:

> *Brethren are unlikely to invite friends into a lodge*
> *they don't feel good about.*

Unfortunately many lodges have ceased to feel good; numbers are low; visitors are few; the ritual is poor and the festive board a quiet affair which finishes early — but there's no need for this. You can feel good — and the good news is that it's not that hard.

In this book you will find a lot of exciting stuff to do even without a candidate and, oddly enough, doing this sort of thing will actually bring candidates. I'll explain *the law of paradoxical intent* later but for now:

> *The more that a lodge feels good about itself,*
> *the more likely it is to attract candidates.*

Of course, learning how to feel good requires doing something different. After all, doing the *same old, same old* won't achieve anything, but change is not always easy. Declining lodges are usually run by a small group of older brethren, doing their their level best. Carrying the lodge for a number of years, they now have just enough energy to do what they've always done — but not much more. They are not looking for new ideas and may even resist them. Just to contemplate them requires energy they do not have and such ideas may be seen as criticism of wonderful masons who have served the lodge loyally.

So change in a failing lodge cannot be made all at once. It is like the old story of how to eat an elephant — one bite at a time — but once the first change is made the next is easier, because when change starts whatever energy there is in the lodge coalesces around it.

The response to change is almost always the same. 10% are immediately for it and 10% immediately against. 80% are not sure; some think it might be OK and some think it might not. Trying to convince the 10% against is a waste of time but if you convince a third of the waverers, the change makes itself.

The reward? In the last three years, our lodge has received:

- *50 enquiries regarding membership.*
- *34 of whom responded to our initial contact.*
- *16 of whom came to meet us face to face.*
- *14 of whom joined us (3 joining members and 11 initiates.)*

Of the 50 initial enquiries, 47 were from strangers. As I write, there are 10 candidates on our waiting list, so there is a truth I want you to accept:

There are many men out there anxious to become members.
They simply have not found a friendly way in.

As you read this book, remember that St Laurence Lodge is a normal, provincial lodge and its membership is probably typical of most lodges under the banner of the United Grand Lodge of England.

Bro. Chris, our paterfamilias, *who quietly assists all our ventures.*

Easy changes

In a manner of speaking, semantics won't do,
In this life that we live, we only make do.
Winston Tong. Sung by Nouvelle Vague

Success will breed success but take it easy. Start with those areas which are not sacred and become more ambitious only later. An example? Well, changes to improve talks and the festive board are unlikely to cause much dissension — and they can have quick results.

Improving talks

The truth is that during a typical talk, 10% of the audience is quite interested, 20% mildly interested, 30% enjoy bits — and the rest are comatose. Lectures and talks are a one-way form of communication, from speaker to audience. The speaker is active, giving information, while the audience is passive, receiving it — and as Masons, we are not used to this. One of the strengths of our Masonic ceremonies is that the audience, the lodge itself, is always actively involved, if only in rising, giving signs and joining in song.

Talks are too often just a matter of words and *in a manner of speaking, semantics won't do*. In normal life, and certainly in Masonic life, we are used to more than just words. Television is a visual and a verbal experience. Our ritual adds participation and action — another reason why it works so well. We should recognise that one-way, single track communication will not hold attention in lodge.

Indeed, one might set out some rules for talks in lodge. They should:

- be of real interest to more than 50% of the audience and be of general interest to the rest,
- be illustrated by pictures and music,
- be no longer than 35 minutes,
- invite participation, for example:
    - encourage questions.
    - end with a quiz.

Too many talks are of interest only to the speaker. That may be fair enough if a speaker is invited at the last minute but given proper notice a good speaker will reach out to his audience. The lodge secretary will usually know some weeks or even months before that a talk is required. He should maintain a list of speakers — discover who has something to say of interest to the brethren and help the speaker customise his talk for the lodge's needs.

Lawrie and I do our fair share of speaking at lodge meetings and we use what some might call a *multi-media presentation;* music, pictures, video and sound effects. Illustration of a talk is not that difficult, given a reasonable understanding of the technology available. A PC can connect easily to a projector which is not too expensive[1] to buy or hire. Both Apple™ and Windows™ formats have slide creation software. One can find pictures and music on the web[2] or use one's own. (Admittedly, there is a drawback in the amount of kit one has to carry around.)

A good speed for a talk is 100 words a minute. Some advise 125, but with the presence of older brethren in lodge, it is best to speak a little more slowly. A 35 minute talk is therefore 3,500 words. Cramming in more will detract from, not add to, the talk. If a speaker likes to digress, perhaps fitting examples specifically to the lodge as he proceeds, then the number of words must be reduced accordingly.

After a talk, which may have involved the speaker in considerable time for preparation and travel, the few questions come usually from the Secretary who feels duty bound to speak up. All too often the audience has become passive during the talk and finds it impossible to get up the energy to ask a question. If the speaker makes it clear, right at the beginning, that he wants questions, brethren will actively try to find one to ask. This will at least counter that WM who, as soon as the speaker has finished, says something like, *"Thank you Bro. Speaker for that most interesting talk. (Knocks) Item 6, Bro. Secretary."* It happens!

Mike Neville, author of *Sacred Secrets* and a very good speaker indeed, divides his audience into two teams to compete in answering questions at the end of his talk. It is noticeable how things liven up when the quiz starts. Do read Mike's outstanding[3] book and do remember to identify the teams before the talk starts, so that the audience will be active in identifying questions they might be asked.

---

[1] The cheapest new is just under £200 and there is a great deal of choice under £300. They can be hired for about £50 a day.

[2] Being careful with copyright.

[3] *Sacred Secrets*, Mike Neville, The History Press, 2012

Thus a talk or lecture can be materially improved by:
- being of real interest to more than 50% of the audience.
- being accompanied by pictures, sounds and music.
- being the right length and given at the right speed.
- inviting questions before the start.
- and having a quiz at the end.

A quiz

Of course, there's another idea! A quiz at the end of a lecture improves interest in and retention of the lecture — but a quiz can be a standalone entertainment as the main event of the evening. I say, *evening* because a quiz works best at the festive board.

The festive board is set up with each team having its own table. The menu can be less formal than usual, perhaps the traditional pub quiz fare of chicken and chips in a basket. Formal toasts can be given right at the start and the other toasts perhaps during the rounds of the quiz — given the usual format of sets of questions on specific subjects (allowing the joker to be played) with scoring after each round. There might be a marathon identifying pictures of famous Freemasons.[4]

The quiz would be on Masonic subjects, for example:
- Ritual matters
- History of the Craft
- Beyond the Craft
- The lodge itself (mix visitors and members in the teams)
- The Province or area
- Grand Lodge
- The Charities

The meeting itself might feature those parts of the ritual not always performed: opening and closing in all three degrees; the tracing boards, perhaps together with a lecture on the *how and why* of tracing boards; the long closing; the charges in all three degrees and so on. If a lecture is required, choose one to connect with and introduce the quiz to follow. An annual quiz might give the lodge quite a reputation over time and attract visitors, especially if the prizes are worthwhile, including perhaps a significant donation to the lodge charity of the winning visitor.

---

[4] Examples can be seen at http://stlaurencelodge.org.uk/masonic-quiz/.

Improving the Festive Board

In North America, the festive board is a rare event. In English Freemasonry, the festive board is an integral part of the meeting and so it should be handled properly. The food and drink will be what the lodge can afford but the success of the rest of the festive board has little to do with money. It is a matter of management: of thought, creativity and good manners.

The brethren do have to be found a seat. That is no surprise. It is no surprise either that there will be a toast to the Master, nor that he will be expected to respond. Neither should it be a surprise that there will be a toast to the visitors nor that a visitor must be found to respond. These events happen at every festive board and it is amazing that they are so badly handled in so many lodges. A little preparation will make an enormous difference to the success of the festive board — and make the brethren feel good.

- Is the table plan well thought out?
- Have you decided with whom the Master will take wine?
- Is the list of formal toasts up to date?
- Which brethren have been invited to give the toasts?
- Have they been given any advice or indeed training on how to give a toast?
- Has a guest been invited to respond to the visitors' toast?
- Has he been given at least a week's notice?

Table plan

A table plan you ask? It is more and more common for no table plan to be prepared. This is daft. A good table plan will facilitate conversation. Conversation will flow across the table more easily than sideways but both should be planned, taking into account common interests, mutual acquaintances or recent experiences.

A brother must of course be sat with his guests but a guest may share interests with another brother besides his host. Newer brethren can be sat with different brethren at each meeting, helping them to get to know everyone. Grand officers are often stuck on top table when they could be dispersed among those brethren interested in their 'grand' lives — and so have more fun themselves. Don't get hung up on rank and precedence. In a private lodge, good conversation matters most.

Table planning is a minor art form. It can be made more easy by software which enables you to move names around the plan until you are satisfied and then print out something attractive, looking as if you have put effort into it — which you have.[5] Don't miss this opportunity to make something happen, to do something different. It is an easy change to make and is unlikely to upset anyone.

Public speaking

An after dinner speech can be a catalyst for change.
It is an opportunity to speak about Masonry, the lodge and the future.

There is no doubt that the standard of toasts at the festive board has declined. There are many reasons for this but the most obvious is that speakers are so often given little notice. The shortest notice I had was when the Master said, *Brethren, the next toast will be given by W. Bro. David West*. I assure you that I had no idea that I was to speak until that moment. If you want a Brother to give or reply to a toast, then it is only polite to invite him ahead of time. In fact, it is plain bad manners to ask a brother to speak at the last minute.[6]

A good speech gives your brethren pleasure, so it is worth working at it. Do not forget the four P's: *poor preparation yields poor performance*.[7]

How long should your speech be? Ten minutes is a long speech. At 100 words a minute, such a speech would amount to a thousand words. Sometimes even two or three minutes will do. It depends on what you want to say, and whether what you have to say will hold the attention of the brethren. *If you can't be good, be quick!*

Handling your nerves

Remember, in all aspects of life, you have two choices. You can handle the pressure or you can back off. It is so much easier not to try because then you cannot lose. In effect, you define yourself as someone who never achieves – and perhaps you learn to be happy about this. You set your sights low, treat things as a joke and even adopt a comfortably cynical attitude to those who try to do better. That is a pity but it is your choice. However, if it's stage fright holding you back, we can beat that.

---

[5] *Perfect Table Plan* is a popular choice.

[6] In my view it is also bad manners to say that you have been given short notice. The lodge has been impolite but you should not call attention to their faults if you can help it.

[7] There is a vulgar, if more memorable, version of this.

Good and bad stress

We are all nervous when we stand to speak. I have spent much of my life speaking in public: lecturing at university, giving addresses at conferences, running training courses and so on. Three thousand was the largest audience I ever faced[8] but I am still a little nervous when I stand to speak, even in my own Lodge.

Bro. Len in fine form

Understand the nature of nerves and stress. Some stress (*eustress*) is good for performance. You will have heard actors say that they need to be a little nervous before they go on stage and that the nerves give an edge to their performance. Stage fright ensues when these nerves get too much and we doubt our ability to cope. The objective is to overcome this excess of nerves, not stop any nerves at all. (Taking a drink, for example, is usually fatal.) Here are some techniques to help.

---

[8] It was at one of those mega-conventions so popular in Eastern Europe before the wall came down. I don't think that all 3,000 were present all the time. It seemed to me that the audience was continuously coming and going so that the average was perhaps 1,500. It is easier to speak to a really big audience. You cannot see expression on any face.

Mentally rehearse

Watching the Olympics, you will have seen close ups of sprinters before the start, staring down the course. They are imagining the race, mentally rehearsing what will happen. You can apply this to speech making. Work through your speech in your imagination, from the opening right through to the fire at the end. Imagine yourself standing up, your voice loud, clear and confident. Visualise the audience's applause. Realise that the brethren want you to succeed. They're rooting for you. After all, they are your brethren. Your imagined performance felt good, and the real one will go just as well.

Relaxation techniques

Sit comfortably upright and close your eyes. Place one hand on your abdomen. Breathe in slowly and smoothly through your nostrils without jerks or pauses, pushing your abdomen (not your chest) out. Pull in your abdominal muscles when you exhale. Be aware of the rhythm of your breath and the movements of your body. Note how your hand is moving with your breathing. At the festive board, take a moment to remind yourself of the feeling, breathing steadily, focusing on your hand.

Imagery

You can do this almost up to the point at which you are to speak. Choose an image, something calm that means something to you. Focus on this image. Now choose a 'cue' word. Bring the image to mind and connect the cue word to it. At the festive board, before you speak, say the cue word to yourself and relax into the image for a moment or two.

Use a mnemonic

Remember what you are trying to do; give a good speech. Think of success. Think of putting in the effort. Richard Butler, who worked with the British Olympic team, offers the mnemonic PRESSURE.

P repare	psychologically prepare for the occasion
R elax	reduce the feelings of anxiety
E xternalise	you are not the problem
S tay Positive	have confidence in your abilities
S ingle Minded	stay focused on the task at hand
U nite	feel supported by your brethren
R e-evaluate	a speech is not a matter of life or death
E xtend yourself	give your best performance every time

Content

It is said that the first reply to the toast to the visitors was given by Christopher Columbus, who started with the words, *Brethren, a funny thing happened to me on the way to India!*

Now this joke illustrates a couple of points about speeches.

- Did you know, for example, that Columbus actually set out to find the route to Cathay – India and China? His discovery of America was in the way of a mistake. If you know this, then the joke is rather funny. It you don't, it falls flat. One must talk about matters within the knowledge and experience of one's listeners.
- Was Christopher Columbus a Freemason? Of course he wasn't. That does not stop you putting the word *Brethren* into his mouth! Your audience immediately imagines Christopher Columbus standing up at the Festive Board, just like you are doing. For as long as it is clearly a joke, never let the truth get in the way of a good story.

Be relevant

I keep a notebook in my ritual case. When asked to respond to the toast to the visitors, I make notes during the meeting of significant moments: a particularly good examination at the Senior Warden's pedestal; a fine explanation of the working tools; the clarity of the words of the Inner Guard or the smartness of the Deacons. I am noting positive things to say about the lodge's performance and seeking compliments to give to specific individuals (not relying on the summons but checking for stand-ins.) I want to catch someone doing something right.

By the way

It really is *not* the business of the lodge to say nice things about itself. I find it quite objectionable when the proposer of the toast to the visitors compliments his own lodge on the ritual or the festive board. It is up to the responder to the toast to do give the compliments, if deserved.[9] The toast to the visitors is about the visitors.

Preparation

Once you know you are going to give a speech, start working on it right away. Collect some facts. What is the lodge doing? How is it doing? Has

---

[9] Although the IPM cannot avoid complimenting the WM!

12

a brother done something special? Are there family matters to comment on; new honours to congratulate; problems that have been overcome? If you are giving a toast, find out who will reply. You can pick up the phone and discuss what you will say so you come up with a common theme or ensure that you don't say the same things – or worse still, tell the same jokes. If you are replying, the same applies *vice versa*.

Good speeches have a structure. The speaker does not ramble around but has a specific route in mind. Here is one such:

1. Getting started — the opener
2. Creating attention — the hook
3. Saying something worthwhile — the theme
4. Diversion — a bit of entertainment
5. Saying it again — restatement of the theme
6. Conclusion and ending

Getting started

Whatever you do, never stand up and say that you are a poor speaker or you have nothing to say. If it's true, don't stand up at all! Why would anyone want to listen to you? Promise me that you will never do this (again.) It is just giving up; not trying.

Remember your mnemonic, PRESSURE. You can, and will, win. Speak slowly; enunciate clearly. Speak to the person farthest away from you. This means you will automatically set your voice loud enough so everyone can hear. A good trick is to use a very formal salutation. The full one in the Province of Essex would run:

> *Worshipful Master, Grand Lodge Officers, Officers of District, Provincial and Metropolitan Grand Lodges, Holders of Overseas Grand Rank, Officers and Brethren.*[10]

This takes some time to deliver and gives you time to catch your breath. Some people advise the use of a pause with a smile, (count *One thousand, two thousand, three thousand*) before moving into the next phase of the speech — the opener. If you need help in avoiding the dreadful *I am no good at public speaking* trap, you can start by talking about speechmaking. Here are a few examples that might help:

---

[10] I am assured that this is the right way and that holders of Senior London Grand Rank and London Grand Rank are included in this.

> *The amazing thing about the human brain is that it starts working as soon as you are born … and stops working as soon as you stand up to make a speech.*
>
> *As Winston Churchill said, 'There are only two things more difficult than making an after dinner speech – climbing a wall which is leaning towards you and kissing a girl who is leaning away from you.'*
>
> *Speeches are like babies – easy to conceive but difficult to deliver.*

These openers are not the speech itself; just ice-breakers to lead you into your hook and theme.

Find a hook

A 'hook' is something to hang your speech on. Perhaps the most famous hook was used by Martin Luther King in his *I have a dream* speech. He adapted the opening lines of the famous speech given by President Abraham Lincoln at Gettysburg. Lincoln opened with the words:

> *Four score and seven years ago our fathers brought forth on this continent, a new nation, conceived in Liberty, and dedicated to the proposition that all men are created equal.*

Martin Luther King opened his address with the words,

> *Five score years ago, a great American, in whose symbolic shadow we stand today, signed the Emancipation Proclamation. This momentous decree came as a great beacon light of hope to millions of Negro slaves who had been seared in the flames of withering injustice. It came as a joyous daybreak to end the long night of their captivity.*

By his words he brought Lincoln's words into the minds of his listeners and then contrasted them with the reality of today. He went on:

> *But one hundred years later, the Negro still is not free. One hundred years later, the life of the Negro is still sadly crippled by the manacles of segregation and the chains of discrimination. One hundred years later, the Negro lives on a lonely island of poverty in the midst of a vast ocean of material prosperity. One hundred years later, the Negro is still languishing in the corners of American society and finds himself an exile in his own land.*

Note how Martin Luther King repeats the phrase, *One hundred years later*. Repetition is a tool of oratory.

Sources of hooks

I am not suggesting that every after dinner speech should be as dramatic as that of Martin Luther King Jr but the techniques can be applied to all speeches and the hook is the first thing to find.

- Do you have something in common with the previous speaker?

    Brethren, today's work in the temple put me in mind of the first time I met Brother Fred. It was in the old temple before the central heating was put it. Boy! Was that cold in January! Like today, the work was a second and Fred was Senior Deacon.

- Is there an interesting difference in the ritual; something that this lodge does that your lodge does not?

    Brethren, I note that this lodge has the tracing boards in the centre of the pavement and not at the Junior Warden's pedestal.

- Perhaps a joke which can be picked up later as a serious point?

    Brethren, your WM is a man always ready to take a risk. I remember back in 2007, in fact July 7, 2007 – the 7th day of the 7th month, 2007 – he awoke at 7 minutes past 7. At breakfast he noted that there was a 7 o'clock at Windsor races and that there were 7 horses in it. Obviously a sign! He went straight round to the bookies and put £777.77 on the horse number 7 to win. Brethren, he should not have been surprised that the horse (pause to let someone answer if they can) came 7th.[11]

- Can you use something in the news? Steer away from politics or religion of course but less controversial matters can be useful, sometimes serious and sometimes less serious.

    Brethren, when I heard about the transfer of Bobby Roberts to Chelsea for £20 million, I thought for a moment that it was your Inner Guard that they were talking about. £20 million, brethren? We could let you have two deacons for that!

Developing the hook – the theme

Once you have established the hook, develop it into something Masonic. Your speech should offer your listeners something to think about. This is

---

[11] This story is taken from Yasha Beresiner's little book, *The Freemason's Handbook of Toasts, Speeches and Responses*, Lewis Masonic, 2009. Well worth the £5.99 it costs.

your theme. Here are some examples, using the hooks above, of how hooks develop into themes.

> *Of course brethren, while it may be cold outside, visiting is about the warmth of the welcome …*

> *That of course reminds us that the TB is the relic of the 'Lodge' as it was then called, a drawing on the floor of the room. Ritual does change despite the 'no innovation' rule …*

> *While not exactly advising the Lodge to put its shirt on a runner at Windsor, I do wonder whether we play too safe in Freemasonry. Should we not, especially at our Festive Boards, try to do something occasionally a little different …*

> *Younger brethren are the future of Freemasonry and while I do not really suggest we go out and buy them, we do perhaps need to make special efforts today …*

The diversion

You open and get going; you go into your hook and develop into your theme. However, a good speech somehow always takes a diversion. It serves to emphasise your theme when you come back to it. What is a diversion? Well, often it is a joke.

Using jokes

Never make a series of unrelated jokes unless you are doing a comic turn. If you are, you had better be good at it. Most people aren't. Use a joke that fits the mood of the evening, and never one that belittles or criticises anyone. Avoid smut on such occasions. Test your joke out on your friends and family first. If they are not amused, find a different one.

A joke is a diversion but introduce it as if it were part of the theme. *Bridge* to it; a term from TV and radio, a way of leading to the next item. Never telegraph a joke. Let it be a surprise.

In Yasha Beresiner's book, you can see how he uses jokes within the theme of the speech. Here is one example, slightly modified:

> *Visiting has continued as an important part of Masonry since those early days in all Lodges; those fully open to all and those that draw their membership from a particular school, university or profession. The Bank of England Lodge, however, is having its problems in the present economic climate. As a visitor I was listening to two of the brethren talking and one said, 'We are*

looking for a bank manager.' 'I thought you employed a new manager just a couple of weeks ago,' the other replied. 'Yes, we did,' said the first, 'He is the one we are looking for.'

It is a gentle joke but what makes it work is the way that it appears in the speech. When would the audience have been first aware that a joke was being told? Possibly not until the punch line.

Bro. Bob, one of the funniest speakers in Freemasonry.

There are websites for jokes, books galore. Be careful to select your joke carefully and then re-word it so that it fits your speech pattern. Here is a story with a moral.

One evening a businessman on a road trip called in at a bar. He asked the barman for a pint and then turned to view the room. Over in the corner was a group having a great time. One of them would call out a number and everyone else would roar with laughter. Someone else would call a number and again they would all laugh – and so it went on.

The business man turned back to the barman and asked, 'What's going on over there?' 'Ah,' said the barman, 'They're a bunch of commercial travellers. They all know the same jokes so to save time, they've given them numbers. One of them calls out a number; they all remember the joke and they all laugh.'

> 'How wonderful,' said the business man. 'Do you think they'd mind if I joined them?' 'Not at all. They're very friendly chaps. You go over and I'll bring your pint.' So the businessman went over, was welcomed and sat down and the commercial travellers went on as before. After a bit, the businessman felt a bit left out and decided to join in. He called out, 'Number 57'. Silence. 'Number 49'. Silence again. In desperation, and remembering that the best ones are the old ones, he called out, 'Number 5'.
>
> In the silence, he went back to the bar.'I thought you said they were friendly. I called out some numbers but they didn't laugh.' 'Ah,' said the barman, 'They didn't like the way you tell'em.'

Telling a joke is never really about the joke itself. It's the way you tell'em. Work at it. It is a matter of timing. The way to learn it is to say the joke over to yourself many times, imagining your audience.

Back to the theme and ending

There used to be an adage in the training world which went: *Tell what you are going to say, tell them, then tell them what you said.* So now you re-state your theme, even with the words, *joking aside, brethren, what really matters is …* Keep this re-statement brief. If anything, this is the most serious part of the speech. It is the bit that you want your audience to remember. Then thank your audience for listening to you. A thankyou goes a long way and this is a signal to your listeners that you are coming to the end — but be warned!

> *Never be tempted to extend the speech at this point. The audience has received the signal that you are reaching the end – and will get very restive if you delay it.*

A speech is like a love affair. Any fool can start one – it's the ending that's tough. As one brother who was hard of hearing said to his neighbour, *Hasn't he finished yet?* To which his neighbour shouted in reply, *Yes, he's finished. He just doesn't seem able to stop.*

Nevertheless, while you are coming to the end, you have not reached it yet. Freemasons are a sentimental lot and you need something heart warming to finish with. Here are some 'blessings' that you might want to use. You can use a couple with the introduction, *And finally brethren,*

> *May your home always be too small to hold all your friends.*
>
> *May your right hand ever be stretched out in friendship but never in want.*

May you be poor in misfortune, rich in blessings, slow to make enemies and quick to make friends. And may you know nothing but happiness from this day forward.

I drink to your coffin. May it be built from the wood of a hundred year old oak tree that I shall plant tomorrow.

May you have warm words on a cold evening, a full moon on a dark night, and a smooth road all the way to your door.

May you have food and raiment, a soft pillow for your head. May you be forty years in heaven before the devil knows you're dead.

… and then sit down![12]

ಙ ಙ ಙ

Bro. Chas can always be relied on for a reply, in England or in Oz.

---

[12] For specific toasts, go to http://stlaurencelodge.org.uk/publications/speeches/

Not lectures but Lectures

Memries,
Like the corners of my mind,
Misty water-colored memries,
Of the way we were.
Scattered pictures,
Of the smiles we left behind

Alan & Marilyn Bergman (lyrics) Marvin Hamlisch (music), sung by Barbra Streisand.

You have improved the talks in lodge and speeches at your festive board, so what next? Well, having talked about lectures (*lower case l*) how about the Lectures (*upper case L*)?

The idea that a *real* Masonic meeting is a performance of the progressive ritual — an installation, first, second or third degree — is a relatively modern view. It arose in the early 19th century following the amalgamation of the two Grand Lodges. That event gave rise to two temporary lodges, the Lodge of Reconciliation and the Lodge of Promulgation, both of which made radical changes to our meetings, one of which was in the way ritual was handled in lodge.[13]

Early lodge meetings

During the 18th century and even before, lodge meetings were quite different from those we are used to. For one thing, they were much smaller and initiates less common. Lionel Vibert[14] says that the brethren,

> ... originally sat round a table with the Master at one end and both Wardens at the other.

If all the brethren could sit around a table, the lodge must have been small by our standards. As the 18th century progressed, the table was dispensed with but meetings still took place in taverns and tavern rooms were not the spacious temples we inhabit now.

---

[13] T.O Haunch, in *It is not in the power of any man ... A Study in Change*, shows that Freemasonry has been constantly innovating. Prestonian Lecture 1972, *The Collected Prestonian Lectures*, Volume Two, 1961-1974, Quatuor Coronati Lodge, 1983.

[14] Vibert, Lionel, *The Development of the Trigradal System*, The Prestonian Lecture for 1925, re-published in *The Collected Prestonian Lectures*, Volume One, 1925-1960, Lewis Masonic 1984.

For a long time, there were only two degrees. There is a lack of agreement on when the third appeared but it was certainly not used with any frequency until well after its mention in 1730 in Samuel Prichard's *Masonry Dissected*, the most famous of all exposures. It was not required by anyone seeking to become Master of a lodge and thus, as was said at the time, *There is not one Mason in an Hundred that will be at the Expence to pass the Master's Part.* The second[15] degree sufficed. Nor was there any ritual, in the Premier Grand Lodge, for the installation of the Master. Colin Dyer writes:

> *In the autumn of 1810, the special lodge (of Promulgation) moved on to consider the ceremony of installing the Master of a lodge. Before this time, there is no record of a general use under the Premier Grand Lodge of any special ceremony of an esoteric character.*[16]

What is more, the progressive ceremonies that did exist were quite short. In the early part of the 18th century an initiation might have taken fifteen minutes, and a second degree no more than ten, if we go by *Masonry Dissected*. Today, in England, an initiation takes about an hour and a second degree 45 minutes (and a third about an hour and a half.)

There is also a view that pre-19th century initiations did not take place during the lodge meeting itself but were worked,

> *... by a minimum attendance, sometimes in a separate small room, before the lodge met.*[17]

Finally, in earlier times lodges met monthly or even more frequently. With many more meetings to fill — but with no installation ceremony, far fewer initiations,[18] only two much shorter progressive ceremonies and these outside the lodge proper — 18th century lodges must have worked a ritual very different from ours. What was it?

---

[15] This partly explains why much of our modern installation ceremony takes place in the second degree and why at the installation *a skilled craftsman is selected to preside in the capacity of Master.*

[16] Colin Dyer, *William Preston and his work*, Lewis Masonic, 1987.

[17] *The Lectures in the Three Degrees in Craft Masonry*, Emulation Lodge of Improvement, Lewis Masonic 1994.

[18] The population of London in 1730 was around 700,000. That of the London Boroughs today is around 8,500,000.

The clue lies in the exposures themselves. They are not ritual books as we know them. The exposures do not provide a script and stage directions so much as a set of questions and answers: catechisms. Some of these catechisms still exist in our ritual. Here is an extract from the *Enter'd 'Prentice's degree* in Prichard's *Masonry Dissected*. It contains some familiar elements.

Q		Are you a Mason?
A		I am so taken and accepted to be amongst Brothers and Fellows.
Q		How shall I know that you are a Mason?
A		By signs and tokens and perfect points of my entrance.
Q		What are signs?
A		All squares, angles and perpendiculars.
Q		What are tokens?
A		Certain regular and brotherley grips.
Q		Give me the points of your entrance.
A		Give me the first and I'll give you the second.
Q		I hail.
A		I conceal it.
Q		What do you conceal?
A		All secrets and secresy of Masons and Masonry, unless to a true and lawful Brother after due examination or in the body of a just and worshipful lodge of Brothers and Fellows well met.
Q		Where was you made a Mason?
A		In a just and perfect Lodge.
Q		What makes a just and perfect lodge?
A		Seven or more.
Q		What do they consist of?
A		One Master, two wardens, two Fellow-Crafts and two Enter'd 'Prentices.[19]

In this extract, we can recognise the examination leading from the first to the second degree. This, with the later examination leading from the second to the third degree, is a hangover from the past, a set of

---

[19] *Masonry Dissected* in *The Early Masonic Catechisms*, Douglas Knoop, GP Jones & Douglas Hamer, second edition ed. Harry Carr, *Quatuor Coronati* Lodge, 1975.

catechisms that formed the main business of lodges in earlier days. Our brethren spent their time reflecting upon the (infrequently held) ceremonies. While an initiation occurred in a side room, in the meeting,

> *... the full Lecture was often worked as an instruction to the candidate.*[20]

The real thing

The catechisms are still relevant and it is a pity that they are so rarely used today. They fell out of use because of changes in the ritual and in the frequency of meetings. The ceremonies of initiation, passing and raising were much enhanced at the union of the two Grand Lodges, such that a ceremony now takes up a whole meeting. While it is possible to carry out a first and a second at one meeting, most lodges are satisfied with a single ceremony, while the third and the (new)[21] ceremony of installation almost always demand a meeting to themselves. Combine this with the current norm of four or five meetings per year and the progressive ceremonies occupy all the available time, *given only one candidate a year.*

The problem is that this isn't always *given*. Many lodges are not finding one candidate a year and thus the progressive ceremonies are letting us down. With their pretence to be all that Masonry is, they make a meeting without them seem like failure. So, to use the jargon, we must turn risk into opportunity. Instead of the feeling that we are failing, let us re-introduce the original ritual of Freemasonry, the catechisms, genuinely offering lodge members an advancement in Masonic knowledge; not a substitute but the real thing.

Obtaining the Lectures

Collectively known as the *Lectures* they are available as:

> *Taylor's Lectures in Sections,* Taylor's Ritual Association.
>
> *The Lectures in the Three Degrees in Craft Masonry*, Emulation Lodge of Improvement.

Both can be obtained from *Lewis Masonic* or any good Masonic supplier.

---

[20] *The Lectures in the Three Degrees in Craft Masonry*, Emulation Lodge of Improvement, Lewis Masonic 1994.

[21] The Antients Grand Lodge did have a form of installation when the Premier Grand Lodge did not, but even this was probably nothing like the ritual we now use.

The Lectures can be seen live at the Emulation Lodge of Improvement which welcomes visitors.[22] While the Emulation Lodge of Improvement demonstrates the Lectures from memory, as did we, there is no real need for a private lodge to do so.

A simple use

The simplest use of the Lectures is to read them aloud from the book. Here is a part of the first section of the first Lecture set out to show the Master asking the questions and the Wardens giving the answers. (My references here are to the Taylor's version.)

> WM *Bro. SW, from a previous conviction that you are a Freemason, I ask you in that character how did you and I meet?*
>
> SW *On the square*
>
> WM *How do we hope to part?*
>
> SW *On the level.*
>
> WM *Bro. JW, why meet and part in that particular manner?*
>
> JW *As Freemasons we should so meet on the one as to enable us to part on the other with all mankind, particularly our brethren in Freemasonry.* (point one)
>
> WM *As a Freemason, whence come you?*
>
> JW *From the W.*
>
> WM *Bro. SW, whither directing your course?*
>
> SW *Towards the E.*
>
> WM *What induced you to leave the W and go towards the E?*
>
> SW *To seek for a Master and from him to gain instruction.*
>
> WM *Bro. JW, who are you that wants instruction?*
>
> JW *A free and accepted Mason.*
>
> WM *What manner of man ought a Freemason to be?*
>
> JW *A free-man, brother to a King, fellow to a Prince or Peasant, if found worthy.* (point two)
>
> WM *Bro. SW, why free?*
>
> SW *It alludes to that Grand Festival given by Abraham* (point three) *at the weaning of his son Isaac when Sarah, Abraham's wife,*

---

[22] The Emulation LOI, founded in 1823, meets at Freemasons Hall, Great Queen Street, London WC2B 5AZ, at 6.15 pm on Fridays, emulationloi.org. On your first visit, you are asked to get there 15 minutes early. Jacket and tie required. Life membership is 10p.

> *observing Ishmael the son of Hagar, the Egyptian bondwoman, teasing and perplexing her child, remonstrated with her husband saying, "Put away that bondwoman and her son for such as they shall not inherit with my son, even with Isaac"* *(point four)* *She spake as if endued with a prophetic spirit, well knowing that from the loins of Isaac would spring a great and mighty people, such as would serve the Lord with freedom, fervency and zeal* *(point five)*; *and fearing that if the two youths were brought up together that Isaac might imbibe some of the slavish principles of Ishmael, it being a general remark in those days, as in the present, that the minds of slaves were less enlightened and more contaminated than those of the free.*

JW   *This is the reason that Freemasons give why all then should be free-born; but, in the present day, slavery being generally abolished, it is considered under our Constitution that if a man be free, although he may not be free-born, he is still eligible to become a Freemason.*

Here we find words familiar and unfamiliar, restoring symbols that we have lost and raising interesting thoughts for a lodge to discuss. For example:

Point One: As Freemasons, we should meet on the square *so that* we can part on the level with all mankind, the one causing the other. Freemasonry *teaches us how* to treat all mankind as equal.

Point two: our Fraternity is universal, without social barriers (*Brother to a King and fellow to a Prince or Peasant*) although Masonic respect is to be earned. Freemasons must be *found worthy*.

Point three: The implication here is that Abraham was a Grand Master. The *traditional history* of our Fraternity is poetic — but not true!

Point four: Was Abraham's wife simply a snob or is there an evil in slavery beyond the captivity of the body? According to this interpretation of *Genesis* 21:10, slavery also damages the mind. This directs our thoughts to one of the benefits of Freemasonry; that *Freemasonry develops the mind*. By supporting and encouraging our brethren, no matter their station in life, we enable *all brethren to grow and develop* when some otherwise might not. It is always a delight to see a shy initiate bloom into the Master of the lodge, able to run a meeting, deliver ritual and give a toast with ease.

Point 5: These catechisms remind us of one of the oldest rules in Masonry; that an apprentice should serve his master with *freedom, fervency and zeal*; the three virtues being symbolised as *chalk, charcoal and clay* which have various explanations. *Chalk* is said to be free because the slightest touch causes a mark. An apprentice may be legally bound by his articles but a handshake, the slightest touch, is enough. *Charcoal* is fervent because it continues to burn even when hidden from view and the apprentice works with commitment even when his Master is not watching over him. *Clay* is said to be zealous because it sticks to everything and the good apprentice sticks both to his task and to his Master.

Which Lectures and sections to use

For our first venture into the Lectures, we used the *first, sixth* and *seventh* sections of the *first Lecture*. This meant that everyone could be involved, including EAs. These sections introduce terms and symbols we no longer use and also explain aspects of modern ritual which otherwise seem mysterious. (I will refer to the Lectures and sections by numbers, so that the first section of the first lecture becomes 1.1.)

Section 1.1 amplifies the questions leading to the second degree but it also talks of the purpose of attending a Masonic meeting; the secrets to be concealed; the words *of, at* and *on* and their meaning; how a lodge is made *just, perfect* and *regular*; and introduces *guttural, pectoral* and a *curious key*. 1.6 expands on *guttural* and *pectoral*, introducing *manual* and *pedal*. It defines *temperance, fortitude, prudence* and *justice* in Masonic terms; explains the *point within a circle* and gives some lovely definitions of *brotherly love, relief* and *truth*, including the passage:

> *Hypocrisy and deceit are unknown among us, sincerity and plain dealing are our distinguishing characteristics while the heart and tongue join in promoting each other's welfare and rejoicing in the prosperity of the Craft.*

1.7 gives another explanation of *chalk, charcoal* and *clay*, another view of the word *free*, and a consideration of the *wind which blows from east to west* in Freemasonry. It also provides beautiful descriptions of *virtue, honour* and *mercy*. One can immediately appreciate the great range of Masonic learning in the Lectures.

A particularly interesting passage is found in 2.2 on the subject of geometry. We usually think of the letter G as standing for God, the Grand Geometrician of the Universe, but it has also stood for Geometry:

> *A science by which we ascertain the contents of bodies unmeasured by comparing them with those already measured.*

Rather neat if you think of rulers, set squares and protractors; calibrated instruments used to measure otherwise unmeasured bodies. 2.2 also contains a description of the six periods of creation, part of which runs:

> *Then, still more to dignify the works of His Holy hands, God created man, who came into the world with greater splendour than any of the other creatures that had preceded him, they having been called into existence by a single command, God spake the word and it was immediately done: but at the formation of man there was a consultation, for God expressly said, "Let us make man," who was accordingly formed out of the dust of the earth, the breath of life breathed into his nostrils, and man became a living soul.*[23]

There is also a passage on the creation of woman.

> *... grace was in all her steps, Heaven her eye, in every gesture dignity and love.*

A later section, 4.1, opens with an explanation of why lodges stand on holy ground and why they are orientated east-west, and then provides an account of the three great pillars. It describes Jacob's ladder and explains faith, hope and charity; three virtues so desperately needed and so little in evidence in the modern world. It describes *hope* as *an anchor of the soul*.

> *If we believe a thing to be impossible, our despondency may render it so, but he who perseveres in a just cause, will ultimately overcome his difficulties.*

Of charity, the Lecture says:

> *Benevolence rendered by heaven-born charity, is an honour to the nature whence it springs, is nourished and cherished. Happy is the man who has sown in his breast the seeds of benevolence; he envies not his neighbour; he believes not a tale told by a slanderer; he forgives the injuries of men, and endeavours to blot them from his recollection.*

There are powerful messages in the Lectures, worth discussion in lodge.

---

[23] The creation of man being a sort of consensus event? Well, they do say a camel is a horse designed by a committee.

Using costume and props

In earlier times, drinking, smoking, dining and singing Masonic songs were very much part of the lodge meeting. While we cannot reproduce this in lodge today, even when called off, the performance of the Lectures can be enhanced by costumes and props. For our first delivery of the Lectures, we hired costumes from a company who supplied amateur dramatic groups. Costumes can be hired from the Royal Shakespeare Company in Stratford. It would be impressive to put on an outfit once worn by a star of the stage![24]

Bros Graham, Chris, Ken, Pat, Trevor and Leslie trying on costumes.

We found wigs and shoes to be the most important part of the costume, since it is relatively easy to furnish oneself with a shirt and some trousers that can be made to look right.

One can set up a table in the middle of the lodge, covering any metallic or plastic surfaces with a tablecloth, laying out some brown loaves, hunks of cheese, bunches of grapes, jugs of apple juice pretending to be beer and bottles re-filled with Ribena. Knives and goblets can complete the scene. One benefit of the mess on the table is that any scripts (in A5 for preference) are not so obvious and the audience may believe that the

---

[24] The RSC charges (2013) about £80 for a week's costume hire, long enough for a dress rehearsal and a performance.

players have learned the Lectures by heart, even if they haven't. The event will be well received as everyone likes dressing up and everyone else (if you see what I mean) happily joins in the fun.

Don't forget the advertising. A line in the agenda on the summons really won't do. To attract a goodly number of visitors, one needs flyers that brethren can hand out to their potential guests. A big audience helps the performance and encourages the lodge.

Older versions of the Lectures

The *Taylor's* and *Emulation* versions of the Lectures are 19th century creations but there are many older versions available. The following is from Preston's *Illustrations of Masonry* first published in 1772. I choose this section for its title, *Brethren cherished*.

Q	*How should you meet a private brother?*
A	*With courtesy and esteem we should hail, but try him and prove him be it day or be it night.*
Q	*How would you prove him in the day?*
A	*By observation of the sign.*
Q	*How would you prove him in the night?*
A	*By the token and the word.*
Q	*How would the wind blow towards him?*
A	*That it may reach him and refresh him under the rays of the meridian sun, should he bear this testimony of claim to our favour.*
Q	*For what purpose should it so blow?*
A	*Favourable it would waft him to a home, be it east, be it west.*
Q	*To what does that wind allude?*
A	*To the influence of that wind which exemplifies the benignity of providence, in the miraculous deliverance of God's favoured people, after their fortunate escape from Egyptian bondage. An easterly wind separated the water of the Red Sea and enabled the Israelites to pass over; a westerly wind made the water return to the former channels and overebbed their enemies in the pursuit of them.*
Q	*What time do you bring to recollection?*
A	*That the sun is ever on the due meridian and in the fixed object of the Mason's admiration; if therefore his claim to our favour*

> *has been proved, it is our duty to screen him from the scorching rays of the sun; enable him to feel its comforts without being injured by its effects.*
>
> Q   *What then is done?*
>
> A   *To the sheltered cove or the cool recess we should invite him, to enjoy the pleasures of our best retreat, hail him with a hearty welcome, ease his fatigues with benevolence and gladden his heart with joy at our friendly repast.*

A little overdone perhaps but Preston, whose name lives on in the *Prestonian Lectures*,[25] wrote to raise the literary standard of Masonic ritual. The first edition of his system was published in 1772.

One can delve even earlier into Masonic history. Earlier exposures give, or pretend to give, the Lectures from much earlier in the 18th century, although the writers may not have always used credible sources. It is argued that *Masonry Dissected* was re-printed so often because it was used by Masons as a ritual book in the absence of any other.[26] In other words, whether it was right or not when published, it became right later!

Using older sources adds to interest and to learning. They contain words and ideas long since lost in our modern ritual books. The following entertainment *Catechism!* draws on such older sources, using material from *The Early Masonic Catechisms*, edited by Knoop, Jones and Hamer.

ಐ ಐ ಐ

---

[25] Preston's Lectures are to be found in pages 159 to 281 of Colin Dyer's book, *William Preston and his work*. The *Prestonian Lectures* originated in the will of William Preston who left money for the delivery of an annual lecture according to his system. This had lapsed by 1862 but in 1924 the *Prestonian Lecture* was revived albeit in a different form. Today the lecture can be on any Masonic subject.

[26] The first modern ritual book was itself an exposure, in the sense that it was published by a non-Mason, Richard Carlile, in 1825, apparently while he was in prison. He was an activist, supporting universal suffrage and the freedom of the press.

Catechism!

First performed by members and guests of St Laurence Lodge No. 5511, the Master being W. Bro. Ed Fehler.

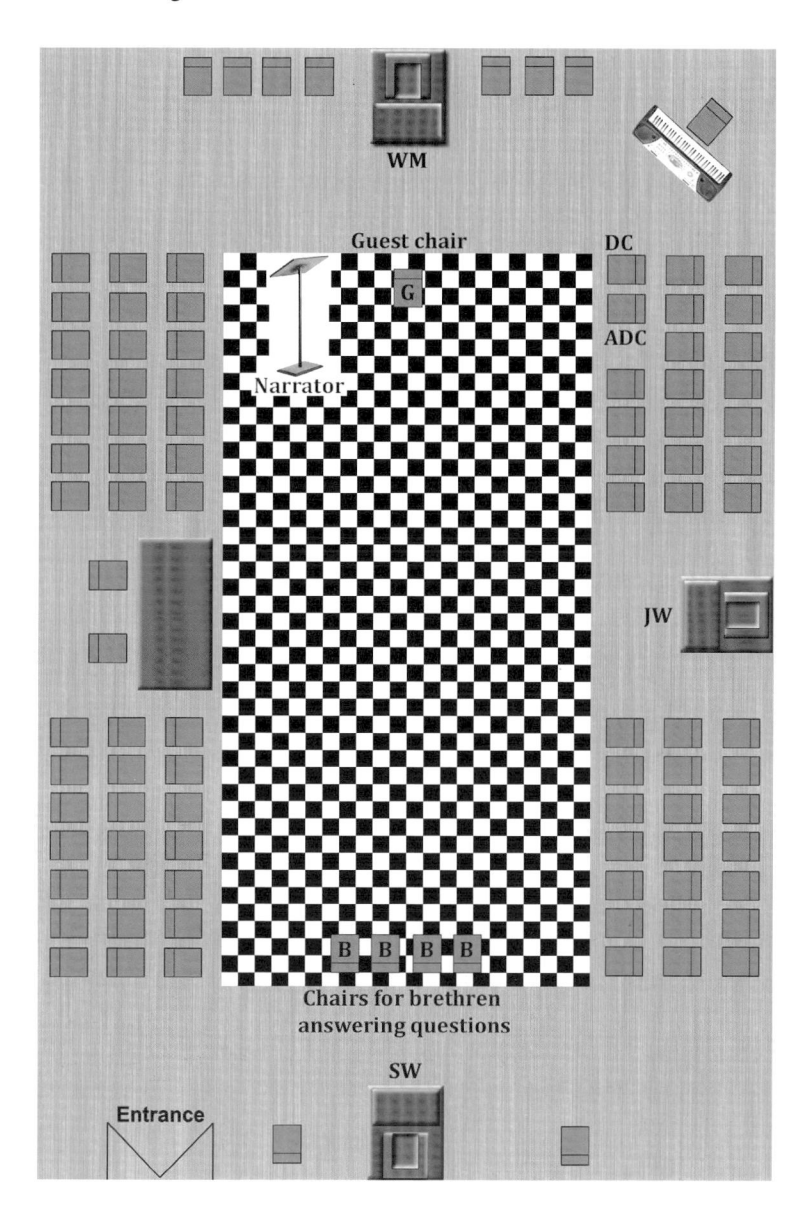

Performance notes

Catechism! is a series of question-and-answer sequences. The questions are read by the WM, the Wardens and others (referred to in the script as guests 1, 2 and 3) who might be lodge members or visitors. The answers are read by brethren in teams of four. For example, in the first sequence the Master and Senior Warden read the questions which are answered by brethren identified as B1, B2, B3, B4.

Chairs for the answering team are lined up in the West. The DC and ADC bring out and remove each team of four in turn while the Narrator is speaking. Thus, at the end of its sequence, team B1-B4 is returned to its seats by the DC and ADC who then bring out the next team B5-B8 to answer its questions in sequence and so on. It helps if teams are seated together in the lodge and if the Q&A sequence is marked up in the script for each team, using a highlighter pen.

To accommodate the guest questioners, a chair is placed immediately in front of the WM's pedestal. The Wardens lead their sequences from their own pedestals. There are two sequences answered by lodge officers who remain in their normal places. The Narrator stands in the North East and acts as a Master of Ceremonies. His introductions give the DC and ADC time to change the teams over.

Remember that this is not ritual. The words and rubric can be adapted as required. The purpose is to inform and amuse.

ಜಾ ಜಾ ಜಾ

Narrator   In the early days of Freemasonry, lodges were quite small, perhaps ten brethren meeting in a room in a tavern. They sat around a table with their food, wine and pipes and worked the Lectures, guided by the Worshipful Master and breaking off at intervals for a song.

Initiations, known as *makings*, were infrequent. The normal work was to moralise on Masonry, that is draw moral lessons from it, working the Lectures. We have an echo of this in the Charge after Passing:

As a craftsman, in our private assemblies you may offer your sentiments and opinions on such subjects as are regularly introduced in the Lecture, under the superintendence of an experienced Master who will guard the Landmarks against encroachment.

32

	The Lectures started out as fairly simple catechisms – questions and answers. Over time they grew until many of the answers became Lectures in themselves. Today, we will demonstrate some of the catechisms, new and old.
DC	To answer the questions in the catechisms, we will invite brethren, four at a time, to come forward and take seats in the West. At the end of each sequence, we will invite another team of four to come forward.
	Brethren who have volunteered will have received copies of a sequence of questions-and-answers and the answers they are to give have been highlighted. The first four brethren are shown as B1 to B4; the next four B5 to B8 and so on. Please be guided by me and by the Assistant Director of Ceremonies.

DC and ADC seat first team, B1 to B4, in the chairs.

Narrator	Be careful how you read the answers, brethren. Sometimes what you read may look like modern day ritual but the words are subtly different. Here we go.
	To start with, we have two sections about the examination of a Freemason, *when properly called upon*. Today such an examination is a rare event — even though we mention it in the questions leading from the first to the second degree. In earlier times, before certificates existed, examinations were more frequent — and more necessary.

First sequence *(B1 – B4 in the chairs)*

WM	Bro. *(using name of B1)*, are you a Mason?
B1	I am so taken and received among the fellows and brothers.
WM	How do you know yourself to be a Mason?
B2	By the regularity of my initiation, by repeated trials and approbations and by my readiness to undergo an examination when duly called for.
WM	How do you make yourself known as a Mason to others?
B3	By signs, by tokens and by perfect points of entrance.
WM	What are signs?
B4	Squares, levels and perpendiculars regularly given which Masons will always honour and obey.
WM	What are tokens?

B1	Regular friendly grips of the hand, mutually given and received, which distinguish Masons in the clearest day as well as in the darkest night.
WM	What are points of entrance?
B2	Those are secrets which I am bound to conceal.
WM	What is their number?
B3	They are innumerable but three are generally known.
WM	Name those three.
B4	With you reciprocally I have no objection.
WM	Will you begin.
B1	Of, at, on.
Narrator	The phrase *Of, at and on* is what is called a 'catch' answer, one that only a fellow Mason would be able to give. A similar 'catch' question and answer is:
WM	How old is your Mother?
B2	(*Gives the number of the lodge.*)
Narrator	The answer, brethren, is the number of the respondent's Lodge. So back to the examination.
WM	What does *Of* refer to?
B3	*Of* my own free will and accord.
WM	What does *At* refer to?
B4	*At* the door of the Lodge.
WM	What does *On* refer to?
B1	*On* the point extended to my n... l... b... (*say the words.*)
Narrator	Most of what we have just heard is from William Preston, writing in about 1770. Let us now look back at the *Edinburgh Register House* manuscript of 1696, twenty-one years before the formation of the Grand Lodge of England and 40 years before the Grand Lodge of Scotland.
WM	Bro. Senior Warden. Will you lead?
SW	With pleasure, Worshipful Master.
SW	Bro. (*using name of B2*) Are you a Mason?
B2	You shall know it by signs, tokens and the other points of my entry.
SW	What is the first point?

34

B3	Tell me the first and I'll tell you the second.
SW	Hele and conceal.
B4	I hele. *(Sign of EA)* I conceal *(Cuts sign)*
SW	When were you entered?
B1	At an honourable Lodge.
SW	What makes a true and perfect Lodge?
B2	Seven Masters, five entered apprentices, a day's journey from a boroughs town without a bark of dog or crow of cock.
SW	Do less make a true and perfect Lodge?
B3	Yes. Five Masons and three Entered Apprentices.
SW	Does no less?
B4	The more the merrier. The fewer the better cheer.
SW	How stands your Lodge?
B1	East and West as the temple of Jerusalem.
SW	Where was the first Lodge?
B2	In the porch of Solomon's Temple.
SW	Are there any jewels in your Lodge?
B3	Yes, three: Perpend Esler, a Square Pavement and a broad oval.
SW	Where shall I find the keys of your Lodge?
B4	Three foot and a half from the Lodge door under a green divot; but under the lap of my liver where all the secrets of my heart lie.
SW	What is the key of your Lodge?
B1	A well hung tongue.
SW	Where lies the key?
B2	In the bone box.
DC	Thankyou brethren. Perhaps you would return to your seats. Brethren holding cards B5 to B8 please step forward.
Narrator	The sequence we have just heard includes a number of unfamiliar words whose use perhaps indicates a closer connection to the Mason's trade than we have today or even Preston had in the 1770s. The mis-spellings may also indicate an already declining familiarity with the trade.

'*Esler*' is a corruption of *Ashlar*, and a '*perpend ashlar*' is a stone that has two smooth faces, both showing in the wall, perhaps at a corner. '*Broad oval*' is a corruption of the words '*broached ornel*', a soft white building stone worked with a chisel. The bone box? Well, here is Preston's version.

Second sequence *(B5 – B8 in the chairs)*

WM	Brother Junior Warden. Will you lead?
JW	With pleasure, Worshipful Master.
JW	What is the first lesson taught in Masonry?
B5	It is the virtue of secrecy and the advantages we may derive from the observance of that virtue.
JW	Where are our secrets kept?
B6	In a safe repository, the heart.
JW	To whom do we reveal them?
B7	To Freemasons only.
JW	How do we reveal them?
B8	By particular signs, particular tokens and particular words.
JW	How do we hope to get at them?
B5	By means of a key, curious in its construction and singular in its operation.
JW	Where do we find it?
B6	In a bone box, secured by ivory keys.
JW	How shall we find it?
B7	We find it pendant, not dormant.
JW	Why so?
B8	That it may be ever ready to defend and never to betray.
JW	If pendant, by what does it hang?
B5	By a sure hold, the thread of life.
JW	Of what metal is it composed?
B6	It is composed of no metal.
JW	Solve the mystery and explain.
B7	It is the tongue of good report in the act of speaking favourably, when justice and propriety require it; otherwise the Mason's chief virtue, silence.

Narrator	The bone box — the skull — contains the ivory keys — the teeth. William Preston was an educated man and his version of the Lectures is a literary creation. He saw the Lodge not as a place of physical labour but as a moral ideal. Here is his description of entering the Lodge.
WM	Whence do Masons principally come?
B8	From the holy Lodge of Brethren and Fellows.
WM	What recommendation do you bring?
B5	A double salute to the Master of the work.
WM	What other recommendation?
B6	Hearty good wishes to all Brethren assembled under his direction.
WM	What is the purpose of your visit?
B7	To rule and direct the passions and make progress in the art of Masonry.
WM	How do you hope to do that?
B8	By the aid of Heaven, the instruction of the Master and by my own industry.
WM	When entering the Lodge, what first struck your attention?
B5	The sun, emerging through the darkness, rising in the East, opening the day and diffusing light, life and nourishment to all within its circle.
WM	Through what medium did you behold this luminary?
B6	Through the medium of the Master, who placed in the East opens the Lodge and conveys light to the understanding, knowledge and instruction to all who are under his direction.
WM	What was the second object that struck your attention?
B7	The sun in its meridian at noon in its full splendour, when its rays are most powerful and the cool shades most pleasing.
WM	Through what medium did you behold this luminary?
B8	Through the medium of the Junior Warden who placed in the South at high twelve invites the Brethren to the shade where uninjured they may enjoy the prospect and regale.

WM	When you depart, what is the third object that struck your attention?
B5	It is still the sun in a scene equally pleasing, setting in the West, closing the day and lulling as it were all nature to repose.
WM	Through what medium did you behold this luminary?
B6	Through the medium of the Senior Warden who placed in the West, at the command of the Master, closes the Lodge, rendering to every Brother the just reward of his merit, to enable him to enjoy a comfortable repose, the best effects of honest industry when they are properly applied.
DC	Thankyou brethren. Perhaps you would return to your seats and the brethren holding cards B9 to B12 will step forward.
Narrator	We are all familiar, of course, with the letter G. There is often a G light in the centre of the Lodge, but do we know to what the letter G refers? Here is the meaning given by Samuel Prichard, writing in 1730.

Third sequence *(B9-B12 in the chairs)*

WM	W. Bro. *(Guest 1's name)* Would you lead?
Guest1	With pleasure, Worshipful Master.

Guest 1 sits in the chair immediately in front of the WM's pedestal.

Guest1	How came you to the middle chamber?
B9	By a winding stair.
Guest1	How many?
B10	Seven or more.
Guest1	Why seven or more?
B11	Because seven or more makes a just and perfect Lodge.
Guest1	When you came to the door of the middle chamber, who did you see?
B12	A Warden.
Guest1	What did he demand of you?
B9	Three things.
Guest1	What were they?
B10	A sign, token and word. *(Gives sign of fidelity.)*
Guest1	How high was the door of the middle chamber?

B11	So high that a Cowan could not reach to stick a pin in it.
Guest1	When you came into the middle, what did you see?
B12	The resemblance of the letter G.
Guest1	What doth G denote?
B9	One that's greater than you.
Guest1	Who's greater than I that am a Free and Accepted Mason, the Master of a Lodge?
B10	The Grand Architect and Contriver of the Universe, or he that was taken up to the top of the Pinnacle of the Holy Temple.[27]
Narrator	So in Prichard's view the letter G refers to the GAOTU, a meaning with which we are all familiar. However, it may surprise you to learn that this is not always so.
WM	W. Bro. *(Guest 2's name)* Would you lead?
Guest2	With pleasure, Worshipful Master.

Guest 2 sits in the chair immediately in front of the WM's pedestal.

Guest2	Why were you passed to the second degree?
B11	For the sake of the letter G.
Guest2	What does that G denote?
B12	Geometry, the fifth science.
Guest2	What is Geometry?
B9	A science by which we ascertain the contents of bodies unmeasured by comparing them with those already measured.
Guest2	What are its proper subjects?
B10	Magnitude and extension, or a regular progression of science from a point to a line, a line to superficies and superficies to a solid.
Guest2	What is a point?
B11	The beginning of geometrical matter.
Guest2	A line?
B12	The continuation of the same.
Guest2	What are the superficies?

---

[27] A reference to Matthew 4:5.

B9	Length and breadth.
Guest2	A solid?
B10	Length and breadth with a given thickness which forms a cube and comprehends the whole.
DC	Thankyou brethren. Perhaps you would return to your seats. Will brethren with cards B13 to B16 step forward?
Narrator	In this passage we see that G stands for Geometry. The second degree, as we know it, is said to lead us to *'contemplate the intellectual faculties and to trace them in their development through the paths of heavenly science.'* There is a persuasive theory that knowledge of geometry, sometimes referred to as 'sacred geometry,' was the real secret of Masonry. Jealously guarded by our operative brethren was the knowledge – the 'mystery' as it was called in the middle ages – of the measurement of angles, squares and solids. Here is more from Preston.

Fourth sequence *(B13 – B16 in the chairs)*

WM	What is the secrecy which subsists amongst Masons?
B13	The art of Masonry, or Masonry and Geometry combined.
WM	What is Masonry?
B14	It is a complete science, which comprehends the system of nature and morals, philosophy and physics, mathematics and mechanics and forms an institution that is wisely calculated to promote the universal philanthropy, true friendship and general happiness amongst men.
WM	What does operative Masonry inculcate?
B15	By it we are taught the proper application of the useful rules of architecture so that a structure may derive figure, strength and beauty from the due proportion and just correspondence of all its parts.
WM	What does speculative Masonry inculcate?
B16	By it we are taught the proper application of the rules of philosophy in the conduct of human life — by ruling and directing the passions, acting upon the square, keeping a tongue of good report, maintaining secrecy, practising charity and every virtue which can adorn the human species.

WM	How are these two - operative and speculative Masonry – connected?
B13	Perfection is the aim of operative Masonry. Happiness is the aim of speculative Masonry.
Narrator	Three, five and seven; numbers common in Freemasonry. Three, five and seven steps. The three grand principles. The five pillars. William Preston, in his *Illustrations of Masonry*, imagines the seven liberal arts inscribed on the steps of the staircase in King Solomon's Temple.

Even though they are not answering in the fifth sequence, B13-B16 remain in the chairs. The officers speak from their normal positions.

Fifth sequence *(Officers 1)*

Note that this is not a Q and A sequence but a series of definitions.

WM	Having passed through the porch, the skilled craftsmen came to a winding staircase that led to the middle chamber where Solomon had ordered all the gifts of merit to be conferred. On every step of that staircase was stamped the name of a different art and over each was appointed a superintendent to try the merit of the claimants to the art.
Secretary	*Grammar* teaches the proper arrangement of words and how to speak and write a language with justice and accuracy according to reason and correct usage.
Charity Std	*Rhetoric* teaches fluency of speech on any subject with all the advantages of force and elegance, contriving to captivate the hearer with strength of argument and beauty of expression.
Almoner	*Logic* teaches the art of guiding reason; to infer, deduce and conclude a train or argument according to premises laid down.
Treasurer	*Arithmetic* teaches the properties of numbers, giving reasons and demonstrations to find any number whose relation to another number is already known.
Organist	*Music* teaches the art of forming concords and composing delightful harmony by a proportion and arrangement of acute, grave and mixed sounds.
Chaplain	*Astronomy* teaches the art of reading the celestial hemispheres by observing the motion, measuring the

	distances, comprehending the magnitudes and calculating the periods and eclipses of heavenly bodies.
Narrator	Freemasonry is a system of morality veiled in allegory and illustrated by symbols. The allegory is the trade of the operative mason. The symbols are found in and around the Lodge. The explanation of a tracing board and the Grand Lodge certificate are examples of moralising on the design, furniture and jewels of the Lodge.

Sixth sequence *(Brethren B13 – B16 still in chairs)*

WM	How many jewels are admitted among Freemasons?
B13	Six. Three moveable, restricted to the person, and three immoveable, restricted to the employment.
WM	What are the moveable jewels?
B14	The plumb, the level and the square.
WM	What are the immoveable jewels?
B15	The rough ashlar, smooth ashlar and tracing board.
WM	Why are these implements called jewels?
B16	On account of their moral tendency, which renders them jewels among Masons of inestimable value.
WM	What is the Junior Warden distinguished by?
B13	By the plumb.
WM	Why?
B14	Because by that instrument, placed at his breast, he exemplifies his uprightness and integrity in the discharge of his duty as the guardian of the Lodge against the attempts of intruders who may dare to encroach upon the privileges of the institution.
WM	What is the Senior Warden distinguished by?
B15	By the level.
WM	Why?
B16	Because that instrument is an emblem of the equality of his government in the West with the government of the Master in the East so that union is effected in the Lodge to contribute to its durability and strength.
WM	What is the Master distinguished by?
B13	By the square.

WM	Why?
B14	It is an emblem of the moral tenets it is his duty to inculcate, to promote harmony and ensure happiness among the brethren which is his duty to cherish and support.
WM	What moral is deduced from the immoveable jewels?
B15	The rough ashlar is an emblem of the human mind in its pristine state which, rude and uncultivated, is like that stone before it has been improved by pious example and virtuous education.
B16	The smooth ashlar is a representation of the mind improved by culture and civilisation, enjoying all the advantages that can be derived from study, example and education.
B13	The tracing board is the emblem of the book of nature, in which are delineated the designs of an all-Supreme Being. An observance of those designs will lead to the perfection of our system, afford present and ensure future happiness.
DC	Thankyou brethren. Perhaps you would return to your seats and the brethren holding answers B17 to B20 will step forward guided by our Assistant Director of Ceremonies.
Narrator	Here the jewels have been moralised upon – that is, moral lessons have been drawn by a speculative Freemason from the working tools of the operative Mason but we moralise on other aspects of the lodge as well.

Seventh Sequence *(B17 – B20)*

WM	W. Bro. *(Guest 3's name)*. Would you lead?
Guest3	With pleasure, Worshipful Master.

Guest 3 sits in the chair immediately in front of the WM's pedestal.

Guest3	What moral does the mosaic or chequered pavement call to mind?
B17	The variety displayed in the works of nature and the vicissitudes to which the life of man is subject.
Guest3	How is that exemplified?
B18	The pavement reminds us that the days of man are chequered by a strange contrariety of events. Today we may tread the flowery mead of prosperity and tomorrow we may totter on the rude track of adversity.

Guest3	What does that ornament teach us to practise?
B19	It warns us not to boast of any success but to give heed to our ways and walk uprightly and with humility before God. It instructs us to practise charity, cultivate harmony and live in unity and brotherly love.
Guest3	What is the proper covering of the Lodge?
B20	A clouded canopy of divers colours.
Guest3	How is it supported?
B17	By three grand pillars: *Doric, Ionic* and *Corinthian*.
Guest3	Why these three orders?
B18	Because they demonstrate the progress of science through strength, beauty and wisdom.
Guest3	Exemplify the allusion.
B19	When men first reared an artificial shelter, strength not ornament was their object. The first rude column gave rise to the *Doric* pillar, the emblem of strength. The industry of the human mind led men to amend this column with figure and shape, giving rise to the *Ionic* pillar, the emblem of wisdom. A spirit of emulation was excited and each man vied to excel his fellow to further ornament the column giving rise to the finished base and enriched capital of the *Corinthian* pillar, the emblem of beauty.
Guest3	What is the grand moral?
B20	When we fix our eyes on the celestial firmament and contemplate the beauties there displayed, we behold the wisdom to contrive, the beauty to adorn and the grace to adorn the handiwork of the Creator.
Guest3	How do we hope to ascend to the canopy of divers colours?
B17	By means of a ladder, composed of many staves or rounds but strengthened by three strongest.
Guest3	What are these three?
B18	*Faith, Hope* and *Charity*. Our faith being well grounded, we hope as a reward of our labours to participate in those promised blessings and dispense such blessings to others.
Guest3	What is *Faith*?
B19	The foundation of justice, the bond of amity and the chief support of civil society.

Guest3	What is *Hope*?
B20	An anchor to the soul. For if we believe a thing to be impossible, our despondency may render it so but he who perseveres in a just cause will ultimately overcome all difficulties.
Guest3	What is *Charity*?
B17	An honour to the nature whence it springs. Happy is the man who has sown in his breast the seeds of benevolence. He envies not his neighbour. He believes not a tale told by a slanderer. He is ever ready to listen to those who crave assistance and, from those in want he will not withhold a liberal hand.
DC	Thank you brethren. Please return to your seats.
Narrator	Let us finish by illustrating the three Grand Principles which form the centrepiece of Masonry. The Lectures contain beautiful illustrations of these.

The officers stay in their places, standing to give their answers.

Final sequence (*Officers 2*)

Narrator	Bro. IPM. How do we meet as Masons?
IPM	On the Square. When we meet in Lodge, all distinctions amongst us as men for the time cease.
Narrator	Bro. DC. How do Masons rank?
DC	As brothers to kings, fellows to princes, regardless of situation or circumstance. We are children of the same parent and brethren of the same tie.
Narrator	And how many grand principles do we have?
DC *(again)*	Three. *Brotherly Love, Relief* and *Truth*.
Narrator	Brother ADC. Explain *Brotherly Love*.
ADC	By this principle, we are taught to regard the whole human species as one family, the high and low; rich and poor; sent into this world for mutual aid, support and protection of each other. On this grand principle, Freemasonry unites men of every country, sect and opinion so conciliating a friendship between those who might otherwise have remained at a perpetual distance.
Narrator	Brother SD. Explain *Relief*.

SD	To relieve the distressed is a duty incumbent particularly on Freemasons, who are linked by one indissoluble bond. To soothe the unhappy, sympathise with their misfortunes, compassionate their miseries and restore peace to their troubled breast, is the first aim we have in view.
Narrator	Brother JD. Explain *Truth*.
JD	It is the first lesson we are taught at our initiation and on this grand theme we endeavour to regulate our lives and actions. Hypocrisy and deceit are unknown amongst us. Sincerity and plain dealing are our distinguishing characteristics while the heart and tongue join in promoting each other's welfare and rejoicing in the prosperity of the craft.
Narrator	Finally, Brother IG, give me a reason to be a Freemason.
IG	I can give you many, my brother, but let one lesson suffice. Masonry gives real and intrinsic excellency to man and renders him fit for the duties of society. For it strengthens the mind against the storms of life, paves the way to peace while promoting domestic happiness; governs the passions, meliorates the temper and gives vivacity to social conversation.
	It may be sufficient to observe that he, who cultivates the science and acts agreeably to the character of a Mason, has within himself the spring and support of every social virtue; a subject of contemplation that enlarges the mind and expands its powers – a theme that is inexhaustible, ever new, and always interesting.
Narrator	Worshipful Master, we have glimpsed a small part of the *Lectures* but I hope the brethren will agree that it shows how Masonry is indeed, as our Brother the Inner Guard has just said, *a theme that is inexhaustible, ever new, and always interesting*.

ଓ ଓ ଓ

The law of paradoxical intent

A paradox,
That most ingenious paradox!
We've quips and quibbles heard in flocks,
But none to beat that paradox!
Pirates of Penzance. WS Gilbert and Arthur Sullivan

Interviewing: candidates always bring something new to the lodge.

When lodges have no candidates, they still carry on doing what they have always done. They rehearse ceremonies (even in lodge itself), listen to lectures, install their new Master and plead with the brethren to find new members. The constant pleading and repeated failure just makes the brethren feel bad — if they could bring in a candidate, they would have done so already.

To escape this vicious circle, we must look at things another way. When faced with any problem, our experience provides assumptions and we try to solve the problem on the basis of them. When we fail, we rarely question the assumptions and thus repeat the same (failed) attempts. We need to get away from wrong assumptions — but this is hard to do.

The law of paradoxical intent holds that by doing something different, even the opposite of what we usually do, we will be more likely to succeed; in terms of Masonic recruitment that:

> *Being busy <u>not</u> seeking candidates will actually cause them to appear.*

It was my constant belief, when selling my services as a consultant, that if I put in the marketing effort, work resulted — but *rarely from the direction in which my efforts had been directed.* I might list a number of potential clients who could benefit from what I was offering. I might write to them, specifying how I could help and seeking a meeting. I might get introductions from people I knew. I might get speaking engagements at conferences. I might network and attend conventions. I might create marketing literature to support a sales drive and so on. These are the usual things to do — and I did them, and I did get contracts, but, and here is the main point, the contracts I won were *almost never from the companies I had targeted*.

The truth is that it is *the effort that matters*. Positive results occurred and I did quite well, because I was *pushing at the world*, as I thought of it. The same can be applied to lodges; they need to push at the world.

> *Candidates will come to energetic lodges, that are involved, active and ready for something new — and thus feel good about themselves.*

The reasons are obvious. People will rarely talk about dull, grey lodges that are doing nothing interesting but they will talk about lodges that are busy, exciting and vibrant. That goes for the members of a lodge as well. Members who feel good about their lodge, will talk to friends, relations and neighbours about it; not overtly to recruit but simply because they are excited about the lodge — and excitement is infectious.

Don't just sit there ...

Getting new ideas and using them requires trust. A lodge focused on old ways of doing things, old assumptions, will resist[28] ideas about new ways and its members will need some courage to put ideas forward. By contrast, a lodge that feels good about itself is always looking for new ideas. So, to find candidates, you do not sit there and wait; you do things, you get active; you create excitement.

---

[28] I was asked to talk to a lodge on how we manage to initiate three to four candidates every year. I explained what we did. At the end of my explanation, one of the brethren said, *No, that won't work.*

Let me give you a proof statement. I do not mean to boast but St Laurence Lodge initiates three to four candidates a year. At the end of 2013, we carried out a triple initiation (using a form of ritual we wrote ourselves) and we still had some ten candidates in the pipeline.

We cannot fit all our work into the four regular meetings and the one emergency meeting that we hold, so we borrow meetings of other lodges. We take seconds and thirds out to lodges that have no work — *away days* we call them. We enjoy a trip out to another temple, meeting new brethren and seeing new sights. We do this some four times a year. We are now reaching a point where we will no longer be able to cope with the number of initiates. We will have to discuss inviting some candidates to consider other lodges.

An Away Day at Freemasons' Hall.

It wasn't always so and we have had our share of problems, but our response has been to get busy, to do interesting things and take new initiatives. What we have discovered — and I really want you to believe this — is that there are:

> ...many men out there who want to join us.
> We just have to find a way to reach them.

It was hard work, and remains hard work today, but we now attract candidates we would never have met in the normal course of our lives.

They are usually younger than our existing members with the benefit that the average age of our lodge is now dropping rapidly.

I will tell you what we did as the book proceeds but, as we go, do please keep the law of paradoxical intent in your mind. Doing something different, even the opposite of what you have always done, will generate energy in the lodge — and energy drives success.

ಐ ಐ ಐ

A Charity Ball with a Latin American theme

Charge! — the Antient Charges, the Old Charges and the Spirit of Brotherly Love

Performance notes

The Lectures are a source of entertainment for innumerable lodge meetings but our ritual and its history also provide a rich vein. I had become fascinated by the various charges in Freemasonry. While we are all aware of the Charge after Initiation, one that always has to be given, there are many others, some virtually unknown to Masons, so I decided to create an entertainment on this subject. It was written to be performed at Essex Masters Lodge No. 3256, with myself as Voice 1 and Bro. Ken Cownden as Voice 2. It had a pleasing reception and it was subsequently performed at many other lodges in and around London.

In keeping with our rules about involvement, this entertainment used Bro. Ken's ability to get the brethren to participate and the usual sets of cards from which volunteers read aloud. In this entertainment, there are two sets of cards — blue and green — which are handed out to selected brethren beforehand; a different set of brethren for each set of cards. At one point during the entertainment, the lodge SW and JW are required to speak up and at another the lodge Secretary is asked to read from the *Book of Constitutions*.

Voice 1 and Voice 2 stand at podiums to read. Voice 1 never leaves his podium but Voice 2 moves around to interact with the audience. We used radio microphones primarily to help Voice 2 move about but also to enable Voice 1 to read 'underneath' Voice 2 at one point. The entertainment might be given without the use of such technology, although the use of a bit of 'kit' does enliven things and raise expectations. At one point Voice 2 mentions the *Long Closing* and offers to give it at the end of the meeting.

Script

Voice 1 Brethren, our topic this afternoon is that of the *Charges in Craft Freemasonry*. We hope that you will agree with us that it is a fascinating subject, full of moral contemplation. In fact, one might argue that the Charges are the centrepiece of Freemasonry, the moral content of our Masonic lives.

Voice 2 The word *charge* has many meanings. In today's mercenary world, we are used to being charged for just about everything.

> This is not the Masonic meaning, although most Lodges remind candidates for initiation to bring their cheque books with them.

Voice 1   We can charge a firearm or a glass.

Voice 2   Brother Wardens, how do you report your respective columns?

SW   Fully charged in the West, WM!

JW   Fully charged in the South, WM!

Voice 1   In this sense, the word means to *fill* or *load*. We are all familiar with the charge of the light brigade, the most famous example of the meaning *to attack impetuously*.

Voice 2   I trust that no one here has been charged by the Old Bill lately? No? Good!

Voice 1   This is another meaning — *to accuse*. In Masonry to charge someone is *to lay a command or injunction upon them, to exhort authoritatively*.

Voice 2   So, brethren: how many charges do you think there are, in Craft Freemasonry? Would someone like to hazard a guess?

Voice 2 interacts with the audience to gather guesses.

> Well, there are six obvious ones. Come on, you must remember. In the first degree, we have the charge beginning *It is customary at the erection of all stately edifices to lay the first, or foundation, stone, at the NE corner of the intended building*. Can anyone remember how the next sentence goes?

Voice 2 gets a Brother to quote the sentence that runs, 'You being newly admitted into Freemasonry, are placed in the NE part of the Lodge, figuratively to represent that stone.'

> Well done! We are familiar with that charge but how about the charge after initiation, the one that begins *Now that you have passed through the ceremony of your initiation* ... Can anyone give us the next few lines?

Voice 2 gets a Brother to quote the sentence that runs, 'I congratulate you on being admitted a member of our Ancient and Honourable Institution.'

> Well done again! We seem to be familiar with the first degree but can anyone remember how the charge in the second degree starts?

52

Voice 2 gets a Brother to quote the sentence that runs, 'Masonry being a progressive science, when you were made an EAF you were placed in the NE part of the Lodge to show that you were newly admitted.'

And how about the Charge <u>after</u> passing? Can anyone remember the start of that?

Voice 2 gets a Brother to quote the sentence that runs, 'Brother, now that you have advanced to your second degree, we congratulate you on your elevation.'

A bit tougher on the memory, isn't it? We do not hear it very often. OK, there are two more to go. What about the charge <u>in</u> the third degree? Can anyone tell us how that starts?

Voice 2 gets a Brother to quote the sentence that runs, 'I will now beg you to observe that the light of a MM is but darkness visible.'

And now a really tough one — what about the charge <u>after</u> raising?

Voice 2 gets a Brother to quote the sentence that runs, 'Brother ... your zeal for the Institution of Freemasonry, the progress you have made in the Art and your conformity to the general regulations have pointed you out as a proper object of our favour and esteem.'

Voice 2   Well done brethren!

Voice 1   So far we have six charges. A lot of moral exhortation! Actually, remembering one of the the meanings of the word *charge* as *exhortation*, we could argue that there are more than these six. There is an exhortation in the third degree beginning …

Voice 2   *Now that you have taken the SO of a MM, you are entitled to demand that last and greatest trial ...*

Voice 1   … which reviews the moral instructions and charges previously laid on the Brother being raised. If we also remember the meaning of the word *charge* as *to lay a command or injunction upon*, you might argue that the three addresses following the installation of a new Master, could also be included in our list. They charge the Master, the Wardens and the brethren with specific duties.

Voice 2   So there are at least 10 Charges concerning moral conduct, within Craft Masonry — a *peculiar system of morality* after all. No wonder we are so good! I am reminded of a tale that our good friend and brother Leslie once told us at the festive board. Bro. Leslie was a policeman and he claims he once arrested a villain who, guessing that Leslie was on the square, tried to curry favour by asking if he could *retire to restore his personal comforts*, to which Leslie replied, *By all means, and on your return, I shall direct your attention to an ancient Charge!* The old jokes are the best ones, brethren!

Voice 1   We often refer to these charges as *Antient*. Not all of them are very ancient, it turns out, but the charge after initiation does go back a long way. The late Bro. Harry Carr, one of the most eminent of Masonic historians, quotes a beautiful version of this charge from Smith's *Pocket Companion* published in 1735.[29] It starts:

You are now admitted by the unanimous consent of our Lodge, a Fellow of our most Antient and Honourable Society ...

Voice 2   Let's read this charge together. Earlier, we handed out some **blue cards**, numbered 1 through 6. The idea is that our Master reads card number 1 and the other brethren with blue cards follow on, reading in turn card number 2, number 3 and so on until card number 6 which is the last one. Worshipful Master, will you start us off please?

Blue 1   You are now admitted by the unanimous consent of our lodge, a fellow of our most antient and honourable society: antient, as having subsisted from times immemorial, and honourable, as tending in every particular to render a man so, that will be but conformable to its glorious precepts. The greatest Monarchs in all ages, as well of Asia and Africa as of Europe, have been encouragers of the royal art and many of them have presided as Grand Masters over the Masons in their respective territories, not thinking it any lessening to their imperial dignities to level themselves with their brethren in Masonry, and to act as they did.

Voice 2 ensures that the next brother follows on.

Blue 2   The World's Great Architect is our supreme master, and the unerring rule he has given us is that by which we work. Religious disputes are never suffered in the Lodge; for as Masons, we only pursue the universal religion of the religion

---

[29] *The Freemason at Work*, Harry Carr, Lewis Masonic, 1981

of nature. This is the cement which unites men of the most different principles in one sacred band, and brings together those who were the most distant from one another.

Blue 3   There are three general heads of duty which Masons ought always to inculcate: to God, our neighbours and ourselves.

Voice 2 interrupts here and says, 'To order brethren.'

To God, in never mentioning his name but with that reverential awe which becomes a creature to bear to his creator, and to look upon him always as the *summum bonum* which we came into the world to enjoy; and according to that view to regulate our pursuits.

Voice 2 interrupts here and says, 'Please be seated brethren.'

Blue 4   To our neighbours, in acting upon the square, or doing as we would be done by. To ourselves, in avoiding all intemperances and excesses whereby we may be rendered incapable of following our work, or led into behaviour unbecoming our laudable profession, and in always keeping within due bounds and free from all pollution. In the State, a Mason is to behave as a peaceable and dutiful subject, conforming cheerfully to the government under which he lives. He is to pay a due deference to his superiors, and from his inferiors, he is rather to receive honour with some reluctance, than to extort it. He is to be a man of benevolence and charity, not sitting down contented while his fellow creatures, but much more his brethren, are in want, when it is in his power (without prejudicing himself or family) to relieve them.

Blue 5   In the Lodge, he is to behave with all due decorum, lest the beauty and harmony thereof should be disturbed and broke. He is to be obedient to the Master and presiding officers, and to apply himself closely to the business of Masonry, that he may sooner become a proficient therein, both for his own credit and for that of the lodge. He is not to neglect his own necessary avocations for the sake of Masonry, nor to involve himself in quarrels with those who through ignorance may speak evil of, or ridicule, it.

Blue 6   He is to be a lover of the arts and sciences, and to take all opportunities of improving himself therein. If he recommends a friend to be made a Mason, he must vouch him to be such as he really believes will conform to the aforesaid duties, lest by

Voice 2   his misconduct at any time, the lodge should pass under some evil imputations. Nothing can prove more shocking to all faithful Masons, than to see any of the brethren profane or break through the sacred rules of their order, and such as can do it, they wish had never been admitted.

Voice 2   Thank you brethren. That was beautifully done.

Voice 1   This version of the very important charge after initiation was published more than 250 years ago but most of it is familiar to us today. However, it does not appear in any of the early exposures and may not have formed part of 18th century ritual.

Voice 2   None of the other charges appear either. There is no charge, in any of the exposures — in or after — the first, second degree or third degree.

Voice 1   After Smith's 1735 *Pocket Companion,* we wait for William Preston's 1772 *Illustrations of Masonry*, for another mention of the first degree charge. Even here, the charge is only described, not given in full, and there is nothing in Preston's writings to indicate a second or third degree charge. These charges must be 19th century accretions to the body of the ritual. Nevertheless, what we do find in Preston is the beginning of what we might consider an eleventh charge, the *Long Closing*.

Voice 2   *(Pause and look around.)* Some brethren have not heard of the *Long Closing*? I am not surprised. As I understand it, it is not common outside Taylor's working. With the Worshipful Master's permission, I shall give it at the end of the meeting. So the charges as we know them are not very ancient at all?

Voice 1   It seems not but there is something which is really ancient. The 1762 exposure *Shibboleth* mentions some *most important charges* which existed in *olden times*, one of which runs:

Voice 2   *That no Mason shall be a common Gamester, to the disgrace of his Craft, or a Sycophant, Parasite or Pimp.*

Voice 1   The author of *Shibboleth* goes on to say that in the reign of King Edward III,[30] these charges were revised. The first of the revised charges reads, he says:

---

[30] King of England from 1327 to 1377. A warrior king who started the 100 years war, he was in reality probably far too busy killing people to worry about Masonic charges.

Voice 2 *That hereafter, at the admission of a brother, the constitutions, charges and monitions should be read by the master or warden.*

Voice 1 The author is not referring to the ancient charges that we use but to what today are known as the *Old Charges*.

Voice 2 Another set of charges? We are up to a dozen then.

Voice 1 Yes, indeed. The *Old Charges* or *Ancient Constitutions*, as they are often known, are the oldest element in Masonry and the strongest link that we have to our operative brethren. In his 1986 Prestonian Lecture,[31] Bro. Wallace McLeod, who has studied the *Old Charges* in great detail, says that:

Voice 2 *Texts of 113 copies of the Old Charges have come down to us, and there are references to fourteen more that are now lost.* What were they used for?

Voice 1 In the early days of speculative Masonry, copies were made for initiates and given to them after the ceremony. One copy, known as the *Sloane Manuscript*, was written on 16 October 1646 at Warrington in Lancashire, for the initiation of Elias Ashmole, after whom the Ashmolean Museum at Oxford is named. It also seems that copies of the *Old Charges* acted like warrants of constitution; as if the Lodge was not considered regular unless a copy was to hand.

Voice 2 So, they were really important,?

Voice 1 Yes, certainly up to the middle of the 18th century.

Voice 2 What was in them?

Voice 1 They begin with an invocation to the *Father of Heaven* and describe the seven liberal sciences, one of which is Geometry which they treat as synonymous with Masonry. They give a history of the art, from Noah's Flood, through Tubal-cain, Nimrod,[32] Abraham and his student Euclid.

Voice 2 Accuracy in history does seem to be their strong point!

Voice 1 From Euclid the history proceeds to David, Solomon, St Alban in England and then to King Athelstan and his son Edwin, who is said to have called a great assembly of Masons in 930 AD.

---

[31] *The Old Charges*, Wallace McLeod, 1986 Prestonian Lecture in *The Collected Prestonian Lectures, Volume Three, 1975-1987*.

[32] Grandson of Noah, said to have been the builder of the tower of Babel.

	They give a list of regulations: some on how a Master Mason must administer the trade, *the charges singular,* and others on general behaviour, *the charges general.*
Voice 2	It may come as some surprise to the brethren that King Athelstan plays such a major part. I doubt that many Masons would have have heard of him.
Voice 1	He was certainly famous in the middle ages. Athelstan was the grandson of King Alfred the Great; born in 895, he ruled from 924 to 939 and was the first genuine King of England. He managed to bring together the English of Wessex and Mercia, the Britons of Cornwall, the Danes of York, the Anglo-Danes of the Danelaw and the Norsemen, to create England for the first time. If that were not enough, the Welsh and Scottish Kings acknowledged his authority and he used family marriages to make alliances with France and Germany.
Voice 2	But most of all, he was celebrated as a Godly King:
Voice 1	*Rex pius Aethelstan, patulo famosus in orbe* *cuius ubique uiget gloria lausque manet*

(*Voice 1 continues reading quietly while Voice 2 begins to read normally to give the effect of 'simultaneous translation.'*)

Voice 2 (*audibly*)

Holy King Athelstan, renowned throughout the wide world whose esteem flourishes and whose honour endures everywhere, whom God set as king over the English, sustained by the foundation of the throne, and as leader of his earthly forces. Whosoever you are who look into this book abounding in love, shining with light, read its excellent divine doctrines which the king, filled with the holy spirit adorned with golden headings and places set with jewels and which, in his manner, he gladly dedicated to Christ Church and joyously made it accessible to sacred learning. He also embellished it by adorning its covers with patterned jewels resplendent as if with various flowers. Whosoever thirsts to drink from streams of learning, let him come. Let him, bearing sweet honey, discover these waters.

Voice 1 (*quietly*)

quem Deus Angligensis solii fundamine nixum
quisquis amore fluens rutilans hoc luce volumen

> *perspicis, eximia dogmata sacra lege -*
> *quod rex aureolis sacro spiramine fusus*
> *ornauit titulis gemmigerisque locis*
> *quodque libens Christi ecclesiae de more dicauit*
> *atque agiae sophiae nobilitauit ouans*
> *hoc quoque scematicis ornarier ora lapillis*
> *auxit ubique micans floribus ut uariis*
> *quisque sitit ueniat cupiens haurire flunta*
> *dulcia mella gerens inueniat latices.*[33]

Voice 1 Historical accuracy is not the strong point of the *Old Charges*. Athelstan did not have a son called Edwin[34] and it is most unlikely that there was a gathering of Masons in York in his time. Nevertheless, Athelstan was clearly a mighty king.

Voice 2 Wasn't he credited with building churches and cathedrals? He must have been very popular with our operative brethren if so.

Voice 1 Athelstan was more a warrior and administrator than a builder. His greatest achievements were the unification of England, the establishment of legal codes and the regulation of coinage.

Voice 2 But back to the *Old Charges*. Do we have a version from Athelstan's time?

Voice 1 No, the oldest example we have is the *Regius Poem* from 1390, 450 years after Athelstan.

Voice 2 Perhaps you might read some of this.

Voice 1 Of course,
> *A good wif was there of biside Bathe*
> *But she was somdel deef, and that was scathe*

Voice 2 *(interrupts)* Pardon!

Voice 1 Oh! I am sorry! That was not the *Regius Poem* but the *Wife of Bath's Tale* from Chaucer's *Canterbury Tales*, written at much

---

[33] From the 10th century poem *Rex Pius Æthelstan*, written during his life.

[34] Athelstan, who never married, had no issue. It seems quite likely that he was gay. His father was Edward, son of Alfred and he had four half-brothers. Alfweard died shortly after the death of Edward and Edwin is said to have died at sea six years after Athelstan's accession. Edmund and Eadred became king in turn after Athelstan. The Vikings sought to recapture the North after Athelstan's death and the two younger half brothers fought to prevent this. Ultimately, after Edmund died, Eadred was successful in uniting England once more.

	the same time. Both are products of the great flowering of the English language, which included John Wycliffe's bible.[35]
Voice 2	So brethren, listen to the *Regius* Poem. It <u>is</u> in English but does not sound like it.[36]
Voice 1	*Whose wol bothe well rede and loke* *He may find write in olde boke* *Of grete Lordys and eke ladyysse* *That hade mony children y-fere y-wysse.*[37]
Voice 2	What does that mean?
Voice 1	It starts by saying that those who are willing to look will find stories in old books of great lords and ladies who had many children and no way of supporting them. It goes on to say that they sought a career for their children that *they might get their living thereby, both well and honestly in full security.*
Voice 2	In 1390, they sent them off to be trained as masons? It's a nice thought. The poem goes on to talk about Euclid does it not?
Voice 1	*This grete clerkys name wes clept Euclyde* *His name hyt spradde ful wondur wide.*
Voice 2	According to the *Regius Poem*, Euclid created the science of masonry and also set out the rules of the trade — in a way that sounds familiar to us today.
Voice 1	*Bet this grete clerke more ordent he,* *To him that was herre in this degre,* *That he shulde teche the symplyst of wytte,* *In that onest craft to be parfytte,* *And so vchon schulle techyn othur,* *And love togedur as systur and brothur.* This great writer ordered that the skilled Mason should enable others to become perfect in the honest craft; each should teach another and so live lovingly together as sister and brother.

---

[35] Wycliffe 1320-1384, Geoffrey Chaucer 1343-1400.

[36] While reading Sarah Foot's wonderful book on Athelstan, I discovered that around 1000 AD, the person responsible for ensuring sufficient provision for every place at which the king's retinue stayed was known as the *hordere*. What a suitable name!

[37] You can get some idea of how to read this old English at http://www.youtube.com/watch?v=e0ybnLRf3gU.

Voice 2 So, according to the poem, Euclid[38] laid that foundation stone of Masonry which forms the very strength of our order today — that no one should be called anything other than Brother and all Brothers should be equal:

Voice 1 *For cause they come of ladies burthe.*

Voice 2 It is strangely moving that the very basis of Freemasonry, Brotherly Love, was so beautifully presented in this poem, written over 600 years ago.

Voice 1 The format of the later versions of the Old Charges is different from the *Regius Poem*. The later versions stem from a version known as *the lost original* which was written about 1550. This lost original was recreated by Bro. Wallace McLeod.

Voice 2 So let's read this together. Earlier we handed out some green cards with numbers on them. As before, our Worshipful Master will commence with card number one, then the Brother with card number two and so on until we reach the last card, number nine. Green cards only please. Good? Off we go!

Green 1 The first charge is that ye shall be true men to God and the Holy Church; and that ye use no error or heresy, by your understanding or by discreet or wise men's teaching.

Green 2 And also that ye shall be true liege men to the King without treason or falsehood; and that ye know no treason or treachery, but that ye amend it if ye may, or else warn the King or his council thereof.

Green 3 And also that ye shall be true each to one another; that is to say, to every Master and Fellow of the Craft of Masonry that be Masons allowed, ye shall do to them as ye would they should do to you.

Green 4 And also that every Mason keep true counsel of lodge and of chamber, and all other counsel that ought to be kept by the way of Masonry.

Green 5 And also that no Mason shall be a thief or a thief's *fere*,[39] as far forth as he may know.

Green 6 And also that ye shall be true to the lord and master that you serve, and truly to see to his profit and advantage.

---

[38] Euclid lived in Alexandria in Egypt around 300 BC.

[39] 'Fere' was pronounced 'fear' or perhaps 'fayre'. It means 'friend' or 'accomplice'.

Green 7	And also that you call Masons your Fellows or Brethren, and no other foul name; nor you shall take not your Fellow's wife in villainy, nor desire ungodly his daughter nor his servant.
Green 8	And also that ye pay truly for your meat and drink where you go to board.
Green 9	And also ye shall do no villainy in that house whereby the Craft be slandered.
Voice 2	Thankyou brethren. So what happened to the *Old Charges*?
Voice 1	Once Grand Lodge appeared, a copy was no longer necessary to prove regularity. Because so much of them was fantastical and so much of them concerned trade regulations no longer relevant, the essence of the Old Charges was re-written to become what we call the *Ancient Charges* today.
Voice 2	The 12 sets of charges that we have mentioned. The ones that are not really ancient at all.
Voice 1	Right. However, if you delve into the current *Book of Constitutions*, around page 143 you will find something never referred to in modern ritual:
Voice 2	The Charges of a Free-Mason extracted from the antient records of lodges beyond (the) sea and those in England, Scotland and Ireland, for the use of lodges to be read at the making of new brethren or when the Master shall order it.
Voice 1	These are the very old *Charges General* and are well worth reading. Perhaps, Bro. Secretary, you would be good enough to read an extract from Section Five?
Sec.	The most expert of the Fellow Craftsmen[40] shall be chosen or appointed the master or overseer of the lord's work; who is to be called Master by those that work under him. The Craftsmen are to avoid all ill language, and to call each other by no disobliging name, but brother or fellow, and to behave courteously within and without the lodge.
Voice 1	Thank you Bro. Secretary. So, the message of Masonry is the same, whether the words are from the *Regius Poem* of 1390, the lost original of 1550 or the *Book of Constitutions* of today.

---

[40] Note that these *Charges General* date from before the creation of the third degree. The implication here is that a Mason need only have been passed to the second degree to be qualified for election as Master of the lodge.

	Saving your presence WM and Grand Officers, in the words of the Long Working Tools in the second degree:
	… yet ought no eminence of situation cause us to forget that we are Brothers and that he who is on the lowest spoke of fortune's wheel is equally entitled to our regard.
Voice 2	Those words are still the moral basis of our Fraternity. After all, brethren: *(moves centre of Lodge and speaks from memory)*
	Our order, being founded on the purest principles of piety and virtue, should teach us to measure our actions by the rules of rectitude, square our conduct by the principles of morality and guide our conversations, aye, even our very thoughts within the compass of propriety. Hence we learn to be meek, humble and resigned; to moderate those passions, the excess of which deforms and disorders the very soul; to be faithful to our God, our country and our laws.
Voice 1	Come brethren, speak the words with us. Let us say them all together in a chorus of Masonry. *(Voice 1 & 2 read leading all those brethren who can speak from memory.)*
All	In like manner, our Order should create within our hearts, the amiable sentiments of honour, truth and virtue; it should lead us to shed a tear of sympathy o'er the failings of a Brother and to pour the healing balm of consolation into the wounds of the afflicted. Then the Brother who has thus far discharged his duties as a Freemason may patiently await his dying throb, that awful change which we must all experience when the soul takes wing through that boundless and unexplored expanse, and may the GAOTU then say, 'It is well finished,' and admit us to the Grand Lodge above where the divisions of time shall cease, and a glorious eternity burst open to our view. Such, my brethren, are the true principles of Freemasonry, such, the beautiful tenets of the Craft, and may they be transmitted, pure and unsullied, through our respective Lodges, from generation to generation.
Voice 1	Thank you brethren. Beautiful words — but perhaps they lack the immediacy of the old charges:
Voice 2	*That no Mason shall be a common Gamester, a Sycophant, Parasite or Pimp.*
Voice 1	We thank you for your attention.

The Long Closing

Brethren, you are now about to quit this safe retreat of peace and friendship and mix again with the busy world. Amidst all its cares and employments, forget not those sacred duties which have been so frequently inculcated and so strongly recommended in this Lodge.

Be ye therefore discreet, prudent, and temperate. Remember that at this pedestal, you have solemnly and voluntarily vowed to relieve and befriend with unhesitating cordiality every Brother who might need your assistance; that you have promised to remind him in the most gentle manner of his failings and to aid and vindicate his character whenever wrongfully traduced; to suggest the most candid, the most palliating and the most favourable circumstance, even when his conduct is justly liable to reprehension and blame. Thus shall the world see how dearly Freemasons love each other.

But, my brethren, you are expected to extend these noble and generous sentiments still further. Let me impress upon your minds, and may it be instilled into your hearts, that every human creature has a just claim on your kind offices. I therefore trust that you will be good to all. More particularly do I recommend to your care the household of the faithful, that by diligence and fidelity in the duties of your respective vocations, liberal beneficence and diffusive charity, by constancy and sincerity in your friendships; a uniformly kind, just, amiable and virtuous deportment, prove to the world the happy and beneficial effects of our ancient and honourable institution.

Let it not be said that you laboured in vain nor wasted your strength for nought; for your work is before the Lord and your recompense is with God. Finally brethren, be of one mind, live in peace and may the God of love and mercy delight to dwell amongst you and bless you for evermore.

Attacks on Freemasonry

> *Under attack, I'm being taken,*
> *About to crack, defences breaking,*
> *Won't somebody please have a heart,*
> *Come and rescue me now 'cos I'm falling apart,*
> *Under attack, I'm taking cover.*
> Benny Goran, Bror Andersson. Sung by ABBA

The earliest attack on Freemasonry that I know of dates from early as 1698,[41] written by a real raver! Part of it runs:

> *For this devilish Sect of men are Meeters in secret which swear against all without their Following. They are the Anti Christ which was to come leading Men from Fear of God … Knowing that God observeth privilly them that sit in darkness they shall be smitten and the Secrets of their Hearts layed bare. Mingle not among this corrupt People lest you be found so at the World's Conflagration.*[42]

It is noticeable that attacks such as this tend to use a standard list of accusations, laid at the door of *anyone-different-from-us-who-we-don't-much-like*, again as I said in my previous book. Here is a sample:

> *They recognise each other by secret marks and signs, and they love one another almost before they become acquainted. Everywhere they mingle together in a kind of religion of lust, indiscriminately calling each other brothers and sisters, with the result of ordinary debauchery, by means of a secret name, is converted into incest.*

This is not an attack on Freemasonry. It was written in about 200AD, a long time before our order began. It is from Chapter IX of *Octavius*, by Minicus Felix, describing attacks on the new religion of Christianity.

---

[41] Interesting in that it shows how early Freemasonry reached public consciousness. There must have been a significant number of Masons around for it to be worth attacking the Fraternity.

[42] *A Warning to this Christian Generation* by M. Winter, re-printed in *Early Masonic Pamphlets*, Douglas Knoop, GP Jones & Douglas Hamer, *Quatuor Coronati* Correspondence Circle, 1978.

Some attacks are not so funny and in modern times, the works of Stephen Knight have caused our fraternity some problems. His best known book is *The Brotherhood*, advertised as *the explosive exposé of the secret world of the Freemasons*. It is a silly book but it has damaged Freemasonry. It has led the PR-isation of the United Grand Lodge of England, with its attempts to display Masonry as a harmless if eccentric hobby dedicated only to raising money for charity.

The effect of PR is to create blandness, the response to any question being nothing that could in anyone's imagination cause offence, and thus vacuous. Interviews with sports people reveal PR training at work. The ordinary Mason knows that Freemasonry is much more than a hobby but if such blandness prevails, the fraternity will lose much of its attraction for both members and candidates.

Membership decline

Nearly all voluntary organisations are experiencing a decline in membership: Rotarians and the Townswomen's Guild being prime examples. Golf Clubs have suffered as golfers pay green fees rather than join a club.[43] In North America, the voluntary organisations which have long been the bedrock of community life, have suffered worrying declines: the *Lions* (down 12% 1983 to 1995), the *Elks* (down 18% 1979 to 1995) and the *Jaycees* (down 44% 1979 to 1995.) Membership of the (US) Federation of Women's Clubs is now less than half its 1954 level.[44]

Robert Putnam, in his landmark essay, *Bowling Alone*,[45] speaks of the decline in *social capital*, the groupings that have been the glue of society. His title is taken from the observation that, while in the USA more people are (ten pin) bowling, few now join teams and leagues. The reasons given are many and various:

> Redundancy or early retirement with loss of earnings.
>
> The fear of job loss causing people to work very long hours.
>
> A loss of white collar jobs through increased IT.

---

[43] *Golf International* magazine (issue 122) reports that 2013 membership of golf clubs in England was down 20% on 2006 figures, although the number playing had not changed.

[44] Data from Robert Putnam, in his landmark essay, *Bowling Alone*. His conclusions are most easily found in his book, *Bowling Alone: the collapse and revival of American community*, Touchstone Books, 2001.

[45] *The rise of solo bowling threatens the livelihood of bowling-lane proprietors because those who bowl as members of leagues consume three times as much beer and pizza as solo bowlers, and the money in bowling is in the beer and pizza, not the balls and shoes.*

Increased divorce.

TV and Internet.

End of earnings related / inflation protected pensions.

Loss of community commitment caused by the need to chase jobs.

Both parents working, leaving less time for community activity.

Children's activities taking up increasing time and money.

Gender equality.

The 'me-generation'.

A philosophy of hedonism among the better off.

Putnam lays the blame squarely on TV. One way or another, people today appear to snack on entertainment, taking it when they have a moment. They consume rather than commit. A major worry is that the decline in membership of social groups is mirrored in a decline in voting, attendance at town or school public meetings and even in membership of parent/teacher organisations. As Putnam writes:

> *By almost every measure, Americans' direct engagement in politics and government has fallen steadily and sharply over the last generation, despite the fact that average levels of education — the best individual-level predictor of political participation — have risen sharply throughout this period. Every year over the last decade or two, millions more have withdrawn from the affairs of their communities.*[46]

Freemasonry has not been immune to such social changes and membership has generally declined. However, in our experience, there are men out there willing and even anxious to join an organisation that offers something more than just fun. There remain pockets of growth and these appear to be centred on lodges who are active and open to change but committed to a higher moral purpose.

Freemasonry must not be seen as a hobby, no matter what PR consultants may say. In 2013, the Social Issues Research Centre in Oxford carried out a study of Freemasonry and its place in society.

> *It concluded that Freemasonry is more relevant today than ever before; that Freemasonry provides its members with a*

---

[46] In the UK, the trend voting turnout in general elections is also sharply downward. In recent elections, the highest turnout was 83.9% in 1950; the lowest 59.4% in 2001.

combination of friendship, belonging and structure, so often absent in today's fragmented society; that it offers a moral and ethical approach to life and reinforces thoughtfulness for others, kindness to the community, honesty in business, courtesy in society and fairness in all things.[47]

Perhaps one of the most important books on this subject is *Observing the Craft* [48], whose author, Andrew Hammer, writes:

The true embarrassment we face ... is that of lodges, who, upon facing a natural shrinking of the fraternity, would then endeavour to alter our institution in such a way that it seeks to appeal to those for whom it was never intended, in a pitiable attempt to put bodies into buildings and money into coffers, without any respect for the dignity and the soul of Masonry.

He goes on to say that the purpose of our order,

... is not to be another public charity or fundraising organisation, but a living band of brothers whose own spiritual pursuits are all that are needed to keep it alive.

The importance of Freemasonry is that it is part, and a significant part, of that social capital that Putnam speaks about; the social glue that is so necessary in our society. He says that:

... social scientists ... have unearthed a wide range of empirical evidence that the quality of public life and the performance of social institutions (and not only in America) are indeed powerfully influenced by norms and networks of civic engagement. Researchers in such fields as education, urban poverty, unemployment, the control of crime and drug abuse and even health, have discovered that successful outcomes are more likely in civically engaged communities.

Stephen Knight

A sad character, Knight suffered from epilepsy all his life and died aged 33 of a brain tumour discovered during a 1980 TV programme.

---

[47] Even that does not capture Freemasonry. It is not something done to, or even for, its members. It is something that its members create by being Freemasons. It is a set of common assumptions, of common premises from which the Masonic life is deduced. This is too big a subject to go into here. I will pick it up in our forthcoming book on the management of the lodge, culture and processes.

[48] Mindhive Books, 2010.

His friend, author Richard Whittington-Egan,[49] writes that in 1977,

> ... he had started to have epileptic episodes. 'When I was ten, I was hit on the head by a cricket bat.' The doctors believed that a consequent area of dead tissue discovered in the brain was the causal factor. Recently, his epileptic fits had been steadily increasing in intensity and duration. 'Not knowing why was,' he said, 'rather frightening.'
>
> Martin Freeth, the producer of the Horizon programme, was anxious to show viewers a scan of an epileptic brain, and, knowing that the mark left by the cricket bat accident would show up, chose Knight as the guinea pig. The scanner revealed that this necrotic patch had increased to the size of an egg. Within a week a biopsy had established the diagnosis of a cerebral tumour, and he underwent brain surgery ...

Knight had left school at 18 to become a journalist on local newspapers, in Ilford and Hornchurch in Essex. He published *Jack the Ripper: The Final Solution* in 1976, the success of which enabled him to become a full time author. He blamed the murders on a conspiracy between the Royal Family and Freemasons; one of many daft theories about these gruesome events. He had another financial success with *The Brotherhood (1984)*, wrote a detective novel, *Requiem at Roganom (1979)* and an account of another famous, unsolved murder, *The Killing of Justice Godfrey (also 1984)*. It was just after this that he had an operation which removed much but not all of the brain tumour. He died in 1985. Whittington-Egan writes:

> When I last saw him, Stephen Knight was calling himself Swami Puja Debal and explained to me that he was now a follower of the Indian religious leader Bhagwan Shree Rajneesh, having become a Sannyasin[50] after ending his marriage.... He wore, I remember,

---

[49] *Ripperologist* magazine, June 2002.

[50] A *sannyasin* is form of Hindu monk who wears saffron robes, the colour symbolising that his soul has been freed from his earthly body.

> *a strange dark corduroy cap … to hide his hairless, bandaged head. He carried with him an air of finality.*

Why he chose to write so much rubbish, we shall never know. Was it the tumour affecting his judgement, a desire for notoriety, a search for financial success or simply an incapacity to sort fact from fiction? Although he has caused us so much trouble, I'd like to believe the first of these possibilities. As his friend wrote:

> *Whatever, let us remember him with charity. He was human. He erred. He was mortal. Spare him that small slice of immortality which is the warmth of his fellows' remembrance.*

One might think that Knight's work has now been forgotten, but not so. In 1989, Martin Short had published *Inside the Brotherhood: further secrets of the Freemasons*, a title designed to attract the following that *The Brotherhood* had created. In 2007, he wrote an introduction to a new edition of Knight's book, in which he implies that Knight was murdered, using Knight's technique of accusation by innuendo:

> *… there seems no room for doubt that Stephen Knight's cancer was anything other than natural. The tumour's progress, histology, its response to X-ray and chemotherapy treatment were all normal. But can a natural brain cancer be induced by unnatural causes which cause no visible side effects, cannot be noticed at the time, and are impossible to detect during later tests and examinations? I still don't know the answer to that question.*

He could have asked someone who would know the answer, perhaps?

Two Entertainments

On the assumption that Knight's stuff is still of interest, here are two entertainments which arose from reading his book. The first is *Attack!* and focuses on Knight's accusations about the influence of Freemasonry on the police. In case you miss it, Knight never accuses Freemasonry of having a negative influence on the police or the judiciary. It is worth stressing this point if only because most commentators on the book seem to think the opposite. (Without knowing it, I set the entertainment in the venue in which Knight discovered his tumour, a TV chat show.)

The second entertainment is entitled *Exposure!* Although it was written quite early in the sequence, it is by far the most complex in its production needs. It is about exposures of Freemasonry from the very early days to Stephen Knight and presents a *shock! horror!* revelation.

Attack!

Attack! was first performed by members of St Laurence Lodge No 5511, the Master being W. Bro. Len West.

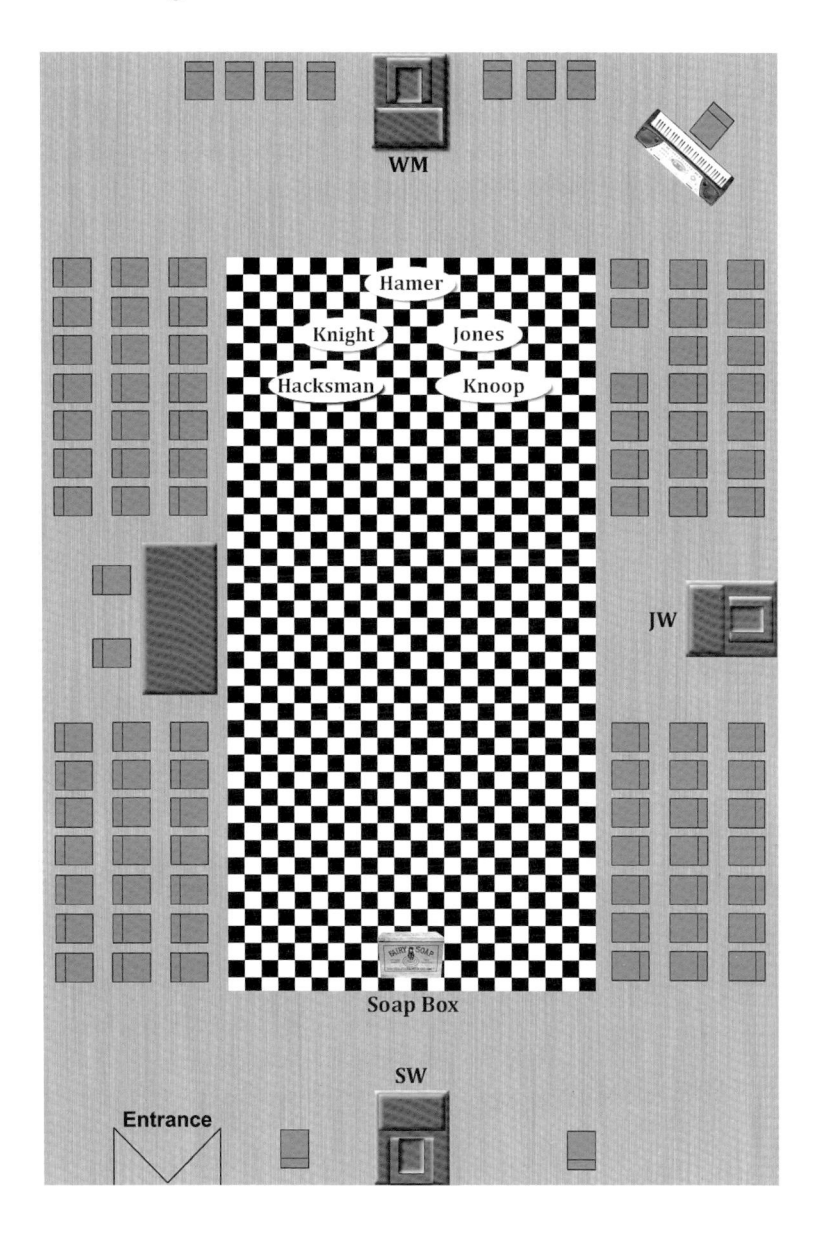

The set is simple; five chairs in the East around a coffee table, representing a talk show set and a soap box, used also as the court dock, placed in the West, facing east. No stage lighting is used.

The Actor	dressed in 18th century costume
Lodge DC	who introduces the programme
Jeremy Hacksman	a television interviewer
Stephen Knight	an author and pantomime villain
Professor Jones	a caricature of a famous Masonic writer
Dr Hamer	another so
Professor Knoop	yet another so
The Judge	played by the WM from his pedestal
Henry Seddon	played by the SD

Deacons, Foreman of the Jury, Clerk of the Court, Warders etc. played by brethren of the lodge.

ಜ ಜ ಜ

(The stewards place a soap box in front of the Senior Warden. The Actor mounts the soap box. The Actor is the only one who is dressed in costume. We must imagine him to be a TV actor, brought in to act out the quotes. He is ever keen to do his bit — in fact too keen.)

The Actor For this devilish sect of men are meeters in secret which swear against all without their following. They are the anti-Christ which was to come leading men from fear of God. For how should men meet in secret places and with secret signs taking care that none observe them to do the work of God; are not these the ways of evil-doers?

(The Actor steps down, bows to WM and returns to a seat in the North West. Stewards set out five chairs facing West around a small table. Soap box stays in place.)

Lodge DC Brethren, that attack dates all the way back to 1698. We will hear from the great Masonic scholars, Knoop, Jones and Hamer about early attacks and compare them with modern attacks on Freemasonry, including *The Brotherhood*, written by Stephen Knight. But first, here is Jeremy Hacksman, to introduce the programme.

Hacksman *(Stands.)* Good afternoon brethren. *(Walks to West)* Let me welcome our panellists for today. Professor Knoop,

Professor Jones and Dr Douglas Hamer. Professor Knoop is a Freemason but his two eminent colleagues, Professor Jones and Dr Hamer are not. All three are respected academics and university teachers. A little applause please brethren! *(As Jeremy Hacksman introduces the readers they stand, nod to the WM and sit in a chairs by the table.)*

Now let me introduce Stephen Knight *(Stephen Knight rises, does a sort of pantomime villain face and then takes his seat)*. Boos, please brethren! Thankyou. *(Jeremy Hacksman walks to East and takes his chair)* Professor Jones, let me start with you. Do the attacks on Freemasonry go back before the establishment of the first Grand Lodge?

Jones   The year 1717, which saw the establishment of Grand Lodge, has been regarded by many Masonic writers as constituting a milestone in Masonic history - Tut! Tut! - though we personally do not share that view.

Hamer   *(Interrupts)* See our *Short History of Freemasonry to 1730*, pages 138 to 139.

Knoop   Thank you, Dr Hamer. To the Masonic bibliographer, the year 1717 is of no special importance. The milestone, if it can be so described - Hmmm! Hmmm! - lies in the year 1721 or 1722, marking the very substantial increase in printed references to Freemasonry.

Hamer   Of the items that we print, eleven belong to the period 1638-1721 and fifty six to the fourteen years 1722-35.

Knoop   Thankyou, Dr Hamer - Hmmm! Hmmm! - It would appear that this is accounted for by the growing prominence and increasing membership of the fraternity after 1721. On 24 June of that year ...

Jones   *(continuing the lecture)* His Grace John Duke & Earl of Montague ...

Hamer   *(interrupts and stands as if to give an academic lecture)* Spelt with an 'e' in the first minute book of Grand Lodge, from which we quote. According to Debretts John, Duke of Montagu, spelt his name without the final 'e' in contradistinction to this distant relative, Anthony Brown, Viscount Montague, Grand Master in 1732. *(Jeremy Hacksman kindly but firmly pushes him down in his seat. He continues to talk, seeming to notice nothing out of the*

	ordinary.) Anderson, with one exception at the end of the historical section of the Constitutions ... *(Voice fades away.)*
Jones	*(goes on as if nothing has occurred)* Marquess and Viscount Mounthermer Baron Montague of Boughton, Master of the Great Wardrobe, Lord Lieutenant and *Custos Rotolorum* of the Counties ....
Hacksman	*(Very kindly and patiently, as if humouring a wayward child)* Professor, please excuse me. Is the point that you are trying to make that Freemasonry was brought to the attention of the public by the increase in membership and because the nobility became leaders of the Craft?
Knoop	Hmmm! Well, er... um... yes, that is what we were saying.
Hacksman	I apologise Professor but time is limited. Could we get to the point? Tell us about the early attacks on Freemasonry.
Knoop	Of course, of course, of course. Professor Jones, perhaps you would ... Hmmm? Hmmm? *(voice trails away)*
Jones	The grounds of the attacks, in so far as they can be analysed and separated, fall under four main heads: - Tut! Tut! - religion, morality, secrecy and anti-feminism.
Knight	*(leaps to his feet)* Exactly, exactly, exactly! More proof to what I have been saying. Jack the Ripper was a Freemason. It was all a cover up ...."
Hacksman	When was this, Mr Knight?
Knight	1888! I have demonstrated that ...
Hacksman	But Mr Knight, we are currently talking about 1721.
Knight	Oh! I know you Freemasons. Hiding behind the details ... *(mumbles to himself and subsides back to his seat)*
Knoop	*(recovering from the interruption)* Hmmm! Hmmm! Indeed! What? What? Under the heading of religion, the earliest attack which we have traced is from 1698 ...
The Actor	*(rushes to soap box and starts to do his bit again)* For this devilish sect of men are meeters in secret which swear against all without their following. They are the anti-Christ which was to come leading men from fear of God ...
Hacksman	*(interrupts)* Not now! Not now! Deacons, Deacons! *(Deacons rise, advance towards the Actor and drag him back to his seat.)* Ye Gods, this place is a mad house!

Knight	What god do you mean? The Masonic god, I presume.
WM	Mr Knight, there is no Masonic god. Masonry is not a religion.
Knight	Now, there you are wrong. *(Jeremy Hacksman appears to be about to interrupt)* No, No, hear me out! *(Stands and walks excitedly towards the West, talking to the audience)* The assurance given to candidates, that the title *Great Architect of the Universe* can be applied to whatever Supreme Being they choose, is worse than misleading; it is a blatant lie! Two thirds of Freemasons never realise the untruth of the line they are fed as to the identity of the Great Architect, because it is deliberately kept hidden from them. *(Turns to face WM)*
	Most of the brethren here today will have no knowledge of this. The true name, although not the *nature*, of the Masonic God is revealed only to those who elect to be exalted to the Holy Royal Arch. *(stands on soap box)* In the ritual of exaltation, it is revealed as *(pauses for emphasis)* Jah-bu-lon! *Jah*, Jahweh, the god of the Hebrews. *Bul*, Baal, the ancient Canaanite god of licentious rites. *On*, Osiris, the ancient Egyptian god of the underworld. This compound figure is the true god of Freemasonry.
Jones	Mr Knight, - Tut! Tut! - this is nonsense!
Knoop	Hmmm! Hmmm! And yet, Mr Chairman, such nonsense has been the basis of attacks on Freemasonry for a very long time. Take the 1725 *Letters of Verus Commodus* ...
Hamer	... the first concerning the Society of Freemasons, the second, the Society of Gormorgons. The letters were reprinted by Gould in his History ...
Hacksman	*(interrupts)* Thankyou Dr Hamer
Hamer	*(subsides mumbling)* volume 3, page 475.
Actor	*(puts on mortar board, pushes Knight off soapbox and climbs up himself. Knight stands aside.)* My belief is that if they fall under any denomination at all, or belong to any sect of men, they may be ranked among the Gnostics.
Knight	*(Moves towards the centre of the Lodge, again talking to the audience)* My point exactly! Gnosticism, cabalism, why not the devil as well?

Hacksman	Mr Knight! Please sit down! *(Stephen Knight ignores him and stands snootily in the West)* So Professor Knoop, you are saying that Freemasonry has long suffered attacks from the point of view of religion? By some with rather less heated imagination than Mr Knight here?
Knight	*(sulkily)* Well, if you are going to get personal about it ...
Hacksman	Professor?
Knoop	*(As if he has just awoken from an academic reverie.)* What? What? Hmmm! Hmmm! Yes indeed. Ah! The attacks have centred upon the fact that Freemasons pray to the GAOTU but not through Jesus, which is the essence of Christianity.
Knight	Ah-ha! See! I told you!
Knoop	*(continues)* Thus, the fact that Freemasonry is open to brethren of all faiths is taken against it. Many Christians have been very exclusive about their religion which they say is the only correct one. Hmmm! Hmmm! This seems to have been the basis of the attacks by the Methodists.
Jones	And - Tut! Tut! - some people, like Mr Knight, mistake openness to religious creeds as the creation of an overarching religion with its own God.
Hacksman	What have been the other attacks? You mentioned the heading of morality?
Jones	Yes. Some of the accusations are veiled, others quite open, and include such immoralities as - Tut! Tut! - sodomy and fornication, gluttony and drunkenness. Regarding the two last, the most outspoken attack is in *Ebrietas Encomium* ...
Hamer	... in a passage that does not appear in the original French and which must consequently be attributed to the editor. According to the title page ...
Hacksman	*(interrupts)* Please Dr Hamer!
Hamer	*(subsides mumbling) Ebrietas* was by Boniface .....
The Actor	*(carrying wine bottle and pipe, leans drunkenly against the soapbox)* We had a good dinner. *(burps)* Westphalia hams and chickens, good plum pudding, not forgetting the delicious salmon, with copious libations of wine and huge walls of venison pastry. The bottle *(waves it and drinks)* went merrily about. The faces of the most antient and most honourable fraternity of Freemasons brightened with ruddy

	fires, their eyes illuminated, resplendent blazed. *(Drinks again, still leaning on the soap box.) (Burps.)*
Knoop	Hmmm, Hmmm! I fear that some of the other attacks are less friendly.
The Actor	*(lustfully)* But Sally Dear's the favourite toast ...
Hamer	Sally Salisbury, of course, the noted prostitute
The Actor	Whose health it is they drink the most *(leers around)* And every Turnkey has a taste Of what lies hid below her waste.
Hacksman	Thankyou, thankyou, that will be quite enough! *(The Actor leers round the room again and returns to his seat.)*
Knoop	Hmmm! Hmmm! Would you like a passage that exemplifies the accusations of sodomy?
Hacksman	No! No! No thank you ...
Knight	*(Leaps to his feet)* But these are minor issues. What about the subversion of the police, of the justice system — and the Masonic murders of Jack the Ripper?
Hacksman	Oh well! I give up. Mr Knight, you had better tell us.
Knight	I will! I will! *(Strides to the West and climbs up on soapbox)* There have been cases of obvious Masonic abuse, several reported to me by men of integrity and standing in the law. There are instances where Freemason judges are influenced by their loyalty to the Brotherhood to act in a way they otherwise would not. They are by their very nature dishonourable and always detrimental to society. Take *Operation Countryman*. The biggest investigation ever conducted into police corruption in Britain, would never have been required if the Commissioner of the City of London Police, had not been corrupted by Freemasonry.[51]
Hacksman	Mr Knight, are you accusing the then Commissioner of the London Police of corruption?

---

[51] Arthur Hambleton, who died in 2014 aged 96, was Chief Constable of Dorset for 18 years and best known for his role as head of *Operation Countryman*, the late-1970s inquiry set up to investigate police corruption in London. He was amazed at the extent of corruption in the City of London, the Metropolitan Police and particularly the Flying Squad. 300 officers were investigated, a number that might have been greater but for obstruction that Hambleton claimed came from the top.

Knight	I am saying that Freemasonry corrupted him!
Hacksman	But how did it do that? In your book, you seem to be saying that the Commissioner was rather too honest and believed rather too much in his fellow man — that his errors came from the fact that he took brotherly love too seriously.
Knight	Exactly, he over-promoted Masons!
Hacksman	Did he make the same mistake with non-Masons?
Knight	Well, yes!
Hacksman	So his only crime is that he had too much faith in his fellow man. That doesn't sound like corruption, does it?
Knight	OK. OK. OK. But what about the judges?
Hacksman	Well, I have read your book and from what I can tell, you give three or four examples of judges being influenced by knowing the defendant was a Freemason. Is that right?
Knight	*(Still on soap box. As the conversation goes on, it seems more and more that Knight is in the dock and that Hacksman is grilling him.)* Yes! Exactly!
Hacksman	*(Walks to soapbox but faces WM)* Let us be clear. In one case, you say that the judge, a Freemason, summed up favourably to the defendant, who *gave a sign* you say that showed he was a Freemason.
Knight	Yes! Yes!
Hacksman	*(Not looking at Knight)* What was the sign?
Knight	I don't know exactly but it must have been a Masonic one!
Hacksman	Why must it have been?
Knight	The judge gave him only a one year sentence while the co-defendant got two years.
Hacksman	*(looks at Knight)* Isn't that a circular argument, Mr Knight?
Knight	What do you mean?
Hacksman	The only evidence that you offer for the sign being a Masonic one, was that the defendant received a lighter sentence. You assume that the only possible reason for the lighter sentence was Masonic and so the sign must have been Masonic. But was it?
Knight	I don't know what you mean.

Hacksman	I am not surprised. *(Walks to E)* The next case you describe is one in which the judge is said to have actually recognised the defendant as a fellow Freemason.
Knight	Yes, another one!
Hacksman	But in this case, the judge gave the defendant a stiffer sentence than he would otherwise?
Knight	Yes! Yes! Yes!
Jones	The judge is - *Tut! Tut!* - supposed to have said that ...
The Actor	*(In gown and wig, stands in front of soap box)* the crime was the more reprehensible because a Freemason had committed it and the defendant had compounded this betrayal of Freemasonry by abusing the Masonic bond of brotherhood that existed between himself and the judge. *(Gives elaborate bow to the audience.)*
Hacksman	*(To Knight)* So the judge was more severe because he knew the defendant was a mason? That doesn't sound like corruption either. Then the case of the poisoner? *(Sits)*
Knight	Yes! Yes! Yes! In 1912, Frederick Henry Seddon was convicted of murdering Eliza Barrow, his lodger. *(Gets down from soap box and sits in NW.)*

(The lodge becomes a court. The WM puts on a wig and becomes the judge. Seddon stands on the soap box as the defendant. The JD stands beside him as a warder. The panel become barristers, turning to face the WM. Other brethren become part of the court.)

Clerk	*(facing the brethren in the North East acting as jury.)* Members of the Jury, have you reached a verdict
A Brother	*(as spokesman stands, speaks to WM.)* We have, my Lord.
Clerk	What is your verdict?
A Brother	*(To WM)* Guilty, my Lord. *(sits)*
Judge	Frederick Henry Seddon, you stand convicted of wilful murder. Have you anything to say why the Court should not give judgement of death according to law?
Seddon	I declare before the Great Architect of the Universe *(sharp intake of breath from the actors)* that I am not guilty.
Clerk	*(Loudly)* Oyez! Oyez! My Lords, the King's Justices, do strictly charge and command all persons to keep silence

	while sentence of death is passed upon the prisoner at the bar. God save the King!
Judge	Frederick Henry Seddon, you have been found guilty of the wilful murder of Eliza Mary Barrow. With that verdict I am bound to agree. There is ample evidence to show that you had the opportunity of putting poison into her medicine. You have a motive for this crime — greed of gold. This murder was a barbarous one; a murder of design, a cruel murder. It is not for me to harrow your feelings ...
Seddon	It does not affect me. I have a clear conscience.
Judge	You have had a very fair and patient trial. I, as a minister of the law, have now to pass upon you that sentence which the law demands, which is that you have forfeited your life in consequence of your crime. Make peace with your maker.
Seddon	I am at peace.
Judge	From what you have said, you and I know that we both belong to one Brotherhood *(pause)* and it is all the more painful to me to have to say what I am saying. But our Brotherhood does not encourage crime. On the contrary, it condemns it. I pray you again to make your peace with the Great Architect of the Universe. (*Pause*) And now I have to pass sentence. (*Pause. Clerk walks up to WM and puts the black cloth on his head.*) The sentence of this court is that you be taken from hence to a lawful prison and from thence to a place of execution, and that you there by hanged by the neck until you are dead. And may the Lord have mercy on your soul.

Frederick Seddon being sentenced to death. This is said to be the only photograph of a death sentence being passed in an English Court.

(Clerk walks up to Seddon who holds his hands out. The Clerk mimes handcuffing him. Clerk leads Seddon to his seat in the lodge. They exchange nods. Seddon sits. Clerk returns to his seat. Chairs are turned round and the TV interview resumes. Knight re-mounts the soap box.)

Hacksman Mr Knight, in your own summary of this case you write ...

Actor *(stands in front of soap box)* ... because there was nothing hidden in the interaction between Seddon and the judge, it remains interesting to the student of Freemasonry only in the depth of brotherly feeling. It tells us nothing of the alleged influence by Masonry in the courts. *(sits)*

Knight *(Sulkily)* Yes, well ...

Hacksman So the Seddon case is not evidence of wrongdoing by Freemasons?

Knight *(Sulkily)* No, but ...

Hacksman Do you have <u>any</u> evidence <u>at all</u> of judicial wrongdoing?

Knight *(Excitedly)* Jack the Ripper was a Freemason! And what is more, this truth was covered up by Scotland Yard. Jack the Ripper was no less a person than Sir William Gull, physician to the Queen and a Freemason.

Hacksman Really? How do you know that?

Knight Contemporary descriptions of the mutilations show parallels with an illustration by Hogarth of an actual Masonic murder.

Jones *(Dryly)* Tut! Tut! Hogarth's engraving is not of a murder but of a public dissection in the anatomical theatre, used for teaching purposes in the 18th century. The first anatomical theatre was built in Padua ...

Knight *(Interrupts)* And what is more, the man actively responsible for concealing the truth behind the Ripper murders was Sir Charles Warren, Commissioner of the Metropolitan Police and one of the country's most eminent Freemasons. He personally destroyed the only clue, a chalk message on a wall near the site of the fourth murder. It read:

Actor *(stands)* The Juwes are the men that will not be blamed for nothing. *(sits)*

Knight *(Gets down from soap box and moves to centre of temple)* When told of this, Warren rushed to the spot and washed the message away. He had realised that the writing on the wall was a Masonic message! So there!

Plate IV of Hogarth's 'Four Stages of Cruelty,' showing the body of a villain being cut open by surgeons in the anatomical theatre, an amphitheatre used for teaching in 18th century universities.

Hamer   In fact, it was not Sir Charles Warren who washed the message away but Police Superintendent Thomas Arnold. He feared felt it might stir up anti-semitic feelings.

Hacksman   The message was not Masonic?

Hamer   It has no Masonic meaning. In his report Arnold wrote:

Knowing in consequence of suspicion having fallen upon a Jew named John Pizer, alias 'Leather Apron', of having committed a murder in Hanbury Street a short time previously, a strong feeling existed against the Jews, and as the building upon which the writing was found was situated in the midst of a locality inhabited principally by that sect,

82

	I was apprehensive that if the writing were left it would be the means of causing a riot.
Jones	So - Tut! Tut! - to analyse Mr Knight's evidence, we find - Tut! Tut! - that Hogarth does not illustrate a murder but a dissection; the famous message has no Masonic meaning and it was removed in case it stirred up anti-semitic feeling; it was not Sir Charles Warren who washed away the writing; it was not done in a rush but - Tut! Tut! - carried out later on the orders of Superintendent Arnold.
Hacksman	Well, Mr Knight, I do not think much of your evidence.
Knight	Well you would say that wouldn't you?
Hacksman	You might think so. I could not possibly comment. *(Stephen Knight sits at the table again)* Why, Professor Knoop, do we get such outlandish accusations?
Knoop	Hmmm! Hmmm! Secrecy. Hmmm! Hmmm!
Jones	Freemasonry has been attacked as sacrilegious and anti-Christian; - Tut! Tut! - as immoral and indulging in licentious acts; as corrupting - Tut! Tut! - the state and government officials. The attacks are based upon - Tut! Tut! - a wilful misunderstanding of Freemasonry.
Hacksman	Well gentlemen, I am sorry but that is all we have time for today. Thankyou for coming on the programme and ...
Knight	*(leaps to feet and interrupts)* Is that all? I must protest! This is another cover up! What about the KGB and Freemasonry, the Mafia, the P2 lodge and the Banco Ambrosia, what about the fact that Freemasonry caused the Russian revolution ....
Hacksman	*(Stands)* Thank you and good night. *(The cast takes a bow.)*

ත ත ත

The background to *Attack!*

Most of the words in *Attack!* are taken from published writing, and much of what the characters say is in their own words. I was becoming an expert on Knight's book at the time and the brethren of the St Laurence Lodge were exposed to great chunks of it. This is somewhat ironic given that Stephen Knight claimed that Grand Lodge had banned Freemasons from owning, discussing or even reading his work — an example of Knight's uneasy relationship with the truth.

In creating an entertainment of this kind, one has to give the characters some personality but I fear that in doing so I may have done injustice to the characters. I don't know whether Professor Knoop said *Hmmm! Hmmm!* a lot, nor whether Professor Jones tutted in disapproval, nor indeed whether Dr Hamer was pedantic with details. I don't even know whether Stephen Knight was as excitable or eccentric as I portray him. My defence is that the book, *Early Masonic Pamphlets*, is very academic and often pedantically so. It is quite judgmental as well. Knight's book sadly shows all the signs of a fevered brain.

The trial of Henry Seddon is famous in Masonic circles. It was the subject of debate between two eminent Masonic historians, Bro. JF Ashby (*Death and the Freemason, AQC* Vol. 108, 1995) and Bro. BJ Williamson. Bro. Ashby confirms much of Knight's description of the case. He tells us that Henry Seddon was initiated in Liverpool, Stanley Lodge No. 1325, but resigned when he moved to London in 1902. In 1905 he is shown as a petitioner for a new Lodge, the Stephens Lodge No. 3089 which meets in Marlow in Buckinghamshire, but as resigning in 1906. He was put on trial for murder six years later. The judge was Bro. Thomas Townsend Bucknill and the key forensic evidence was given by two other Freemasons.

Bro. Williamson, in his response to Bro. Ashby in *Quatuor Coronati* Lodge, further confirms the words we use in *Attack!*, saying that half an hour after the trial had ended, the judge was found, still in his robes, sitting at his table, his eyes red with weeping. Seddon maintained his innocence to the last and over 250,000 signatures were obtained in support of a reprieve, which was not given. Filson Young, a spectator at the court, later commented,

> The trial was remarkable in that there was no proof that Seddon had actually handled arsenic, administered the fatal dose, or that he had any knowledge of the dosage required to kill a person.

Exposure!

In writing this entertainment, I thought I would join the exposure game and expose something myself, that:

The words in the first and second degrees are the wrong way round!

Exposure! was first performed in St Laurence Lodge No 5511 when the Master was W. Bro. Jack Wilks.

Bro. Jack Wilks. A Mason greatly loved.

Exposure! is the most complex of all our entertainments and requires a fair bit in the way of props. We used some stage lighting, a mirror ball and a smoke machine which gave immense fun. It was foot operated and as Narrator, I heeled and toed away with élan! The actors wore an approximation of 18th century English costume which, with the addition of sashes and feathered hats, became French. At one point a floor sheet is used. We made small placards with Masonic puns on them to hand out in the crowd scene. At one point, the WM wears a top hat and at another the Actors draw swords. Toys or wooden approximations will do fine.

Exposure! requires music. We were blessed with a string duo of Bro. Eric Stuckey (violin) and Bro. Wilhelm Martin (viola) both of the Incorporated Society of Musicians Lodge No. 2881. Bro. Stuckey has kindly allowed the music to be included in this book.

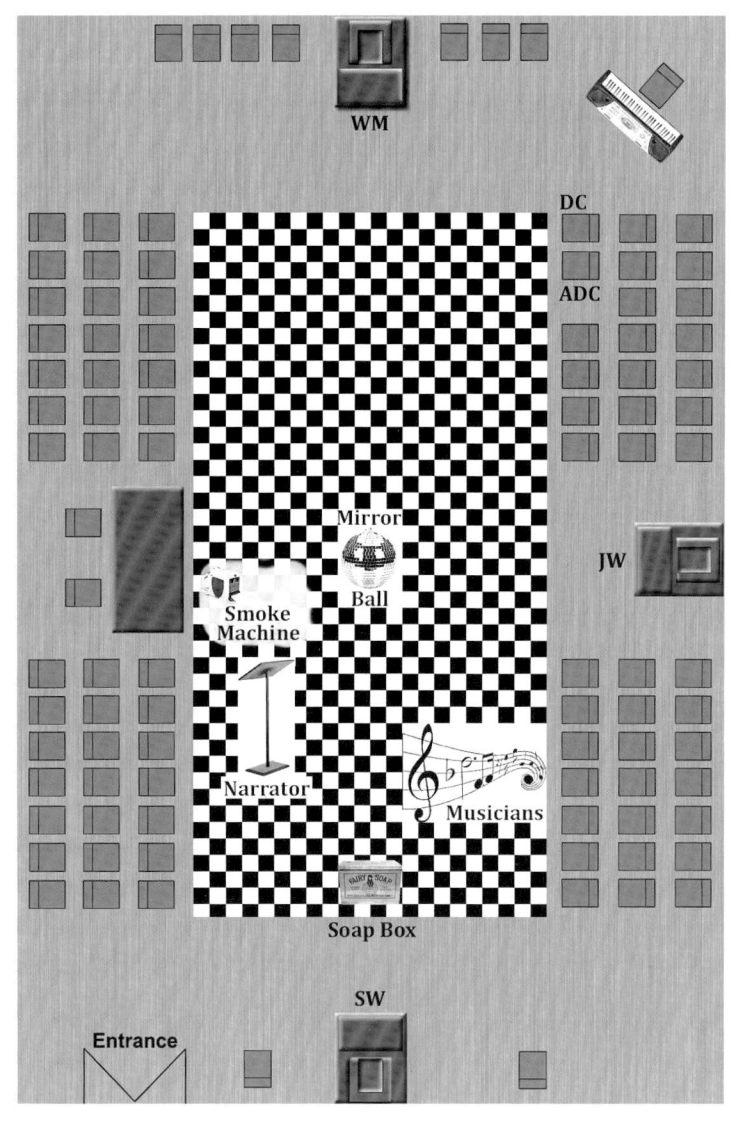

A long time before I conceived this piece, my wife and I co-directed a production of *Oh! What a Lovely War!* — a magical stage event and a pretty good film. It has always stayed in my mind and so some of the stage directions here echo that form of dramatic presentation.

86

The *dramatis personae* are the Narrator who stands and reads at a podium; his on-stage partner the Director, who is in costume and directs the action, and six actors denoted as Act1 to Act 6. Various brethren read from cards as invited. There are several occasions calling for general audience participation.

> *At the start, all lights are out except spot on mirror ball. Music: opening bars of 'The House of the Rising Sun.' Start smoke. No one speaks for at least a minute.*

Narrator: *(Quietly but urgently)* Brethren, *(music stops)* there is an elite group of Freemasons in England over whom the United Grand Lodge has no jurisdiction. The majority of Freemasons have no idea of their existence. Members of Craft Freemasonry often argue that Freemasonry is not a secret society but a 'society with secrets'. No such case can be made out for the wealthy society-within-a-society based at 10 Duke Street.

Quiet but threatening music

Nobody looking at that fine but anonymous house from outside could suspect that behind its pleasing facade, beyond the two sets of sturdy double doors and up the stairs there is a Black Room, (*beat*) a Red Room (*beat*) and a Chamber of Death.

Nobody walking down Duke Street from Piccadilly is likely to suspect the true nature of what goes on inside that building, even if he or she happens to notice the small plate to the right of the entrance which says: "The Supreme Council. Ring only once."

Sharp chord — music continues

> Even the Grand Master of all England is only a Freemason of the 3rd degree and Freemasons are in most cases quite unaware of the thirty superior degrees to which they will never be admitted not ever hear mentioned. This is the real picture, with the three lowly degrees governed by Grand Lodge and the thirty higher degrees governed by a Supreme Council.

Music stops

> Initiation into these higher degrees is open only to those who are *selected* by the Supreme Council. *(chord)* Only a small proportion of these progress beyond the 18th degree, *(chord)* that of Knight of the Pelican and Eagle *(chord)* and Sovereign Prince Rose Croix of Heredom. *(chord)* With each degree, the number of initiates diminishes *(chord)* — the 31st degree is restricted to 400 members *(chord)*, the 32nd to 180 *(chord)* and the 33rd to only 75 members *(series of chords)*.

Quiet but threatening music starts again.

> The Most Puissant Sovereign Grand Commander[52] is truly Britain's highest Freemason whatever might be said of the Duke of Kent. Few of the many hundreds of Freemasons interviewed had even heard of him and, of those few, only five knew of his secret role as the highest Mason of the highest degree.

Director enters and stands in the centre of the lodge.

> Brethren, it is time for these secret leaders to be unmasked. It is time the ordinary Mason knew who was, covertly and quietly, the real power in Freemasonry — those who know the Black Room and the Room of Death — those who are superior even to the Duke of Kent himself. Fearlessly, we will name them.

Music gets louder — triumphant music Narrator has to speak loudly to be heard.

---

[52] Alan John Englefield in 2013.

> Without a qualm, we will force him to step forward into the light — so today, you will know, for the first time, who pulls the puppet strings of the Craft.

Music stops. No more smoke.

Director	Step forward ……………….

Dazzling set of chords. Director names a volunteer Bro. by his Rose Croix title and name. The Director pulls him forward as if he is unwilling to be unmasked. Full stage lights. Brother takes a bow and returns to his seat..

Narrator	The words I have just read were from a book called *The Brotherhood* written by Stephen Knight. The late Stephen Knight started out as a journalist. Nothing wrong with that one may suppose but as the tabloid newspapers stand witness, people want sensation — and he gave it to them. Most of it he made up, basing his imagination on half-digested or deliberately misused odds and ends of fact.

Brethren, this afternoon we are going to explore a little of how our ancient brethren conducted the affairs of their lodges. However, do remember that our material is drawn from published exposures of Freemasonry and may be no more reliable than the rubbish you have just heard, confusing Rose Croix with the Craft.

To be honest, which few of them were, the 18th century exposure writers plagiarised each other unmercifully. Many of them simply copied, word for word, whole chunks of what had been published before. However, they are the only source of information that we have about Masonic ritual of the time and so we must do what we can with them.

Music starts — Beggar's Opera

So come with us back to 1730 to the time of the publication of a book called *Masonry Dissected*.

Act1 enters the Lodge and gives the Director a broadsheet to read. Act1 moves to stand in west.

Director	*(Reads over the music, talking like a Town Cryer, trying to read it all in one breath, ending up puffing.)* Being a universal and genuine description of all its branches from the original to this present time as it is delivered in the constituted regular lodges both in the City and country, according to the several degrees of admission, giving an impartial account of their regular proceedings in initiating their new members in the whole three degrees of Freemasonry viz. Entered Prentice, Fellow Craft, Master to which is added the Author's vindication of himself by Samuel Prichard. *(Music pauses)*

Act1 *(From centre of lodge, tone undercutting the Director)* 29 pages, six pence.

Lights spin. Mirror ball removed. Music starts again — a jolly catch as the actors enter and assemble in the centre of the lodge. Business during the music. Actors walk around a bit, exchange grips and greetings in dumb show, shaking hands with brethren in the front rows, particularly visitors. Then line up, 1,2, 3 in the East and 4, 5, 6 in the West. Actors 1 and 2 walk to the centre of the lodge and exchange the G of an EA. Lights on centre only. Music stops. (For the rest of the entertainment, the Director should feel free to move around the lodge at will.)

Act1 From whence came you?

Act2 From the Holy Lodge of St John's.

Act1 What recommendations brought you from hence?

Act2 The recommendations which I brought from the Right Worshipful Master, Brothers and Fellows of the Right Worshipful and Holy Lodge of St John's from whence I came and greet you thrice heartily well. *(Actors 1 & 2 freeze, maintaining the G of an EA.)*

Narrator The exposure *Masonry Dissected* is the first exposure in English to describe the third degree. Much of what it contains is familiar to us today but much is very different. Whether this is because the author did not really know the ceremonies or because they have changed since his time, we do not know. It is in the form of catechisms — question and answer. Let us work some of these catechisms together.

Full stage lighting. Actors 1 & 2 move back to their original positions in East.

Director Many of the brethren were earlier given BLUE cards on which is printed a number, a question and an answer.

	This is how it works. Our Worshipful Master will read a question. That question will be on one of the BLUE cards that someone here has. The first card is numbered 1, the second 2 and so on. Keep an eye on your card and its number and on the board being held up. When you hear the Master read your question, stand and read the answer. BLUE cards only brethren. The Green ones come later. Here — we will show you. Worshipful Master.
WM	Where stands your Master?
Act4	*(Holds up card 1 and then reads from it.)* In the East
WM	Why so?
Act5	*(Holds up card 2 and then reads from it.)* As the sun rises in the East and opens the day, so the Master stands in the East to open the lodge and set his men to work.
WM	Where stands your Wardens?
Act6	*(Holds up card 3 and then reads from it.)* In the West.
Director	Now it is over to you brethren. The next question and answer is number 4. Who has a card numbered 4? *(Actors look around to find the brother and gets him to hold his card up)* Thank you, Brother. So when the Master asks the question on your card, you will read the answer. Are you ready? Good. Who has number 5? *(Actors look around to find the brother and gets him to hold his card up)* Thank you, Brother. Good! So you answer your question after the brother with number 4 has answered his. Off we go. We will start again from the beginning. WM, please. *(Actors 1 & 4 help by identifying the brethren with the cards. Other actors remain in position.*
WM	Where stands your Master?
Act4	*(Holds up card 1 and reads from it.)* In the East.
WM	Why so?
Act5	*(Holds up card 2 and reads from it.)* As the sun rises in the East and opens the day, so the Master stands in the East to open the lodge and set his men to work.
WM	Where stands your Wardens?
Act6	*(Holds up card 3 and reads from it.)* In the West.

WM	What's their business?
Brother (4)	As the sun sets in the West to close the day, so the Wardens stand in the West to close the lodge and dismiss the men from labour, paying their wages.

As Brother (4) says this, all actors make the sign of F. Act2 places a level on a chord about the neck of Act5 and a plumb-rule on a chord about the neck of Act6. Actors 5 & 6 then take station in the West as Wardens. The Director conducts them to their position.

WM	Where stands the Senior Enter'd Prentice?
Brother (5)	In the South.

The Director conducts Act2 to stand in the South.

WM	What is his business?
Brother (6)	To hear and receive instructions and welcome strange brothers.
WM	Where stands the Junior Enter'd Prentice?
Brother (7)	In the North.

The Director conducts Act4 to stand in the North.

WM	What is his business?
Brother (8)	To keep off all cowans and evesdroppers
WM	If a cowan is to be catched, how is he to be punished?
Brother (9)	To be placed under the eves of the house in rainy weather till the water runs in at his shoulders and out at his shoes.
WM	What are the secrets of a Mason?
Brother (10)	Signs, tokens and many words.
WM	Where do you keep those secrets?
Brother (11)	Under my left breast.
WM	Where do you keep the key to those secrets?
Brother (12)	In a bone box that neither opens nor shuts but with ivory keys.
WM	Does it hang or does it lie?
Brother (13)	It hangs.
WM	What does it hang by?
Brother (14)	A tow-line 9 inches or a span.
WM	What metal is it of?

Brother (15)	No manner of metal at all; but a tongue of good report is good behind a Brother's back as before his face.
WM	Have you seen your Master today?
Brother (16)	Yes, he was clothed in a yellow jacket and blue pair of breeches.

Actors and Director turn to look at the WM in amazement.

Act6	No, brethren. Our Master is not in fancy dress. The yellow jacket is the arms of a pair of compasses and the blue breeches, the steel points of them.

Actors and Director turn back in visible relief. Director stands beside the WM.

WM	Give me the enter'd prentice's sign.

Act1 walks to the centre of the lodge, facing the WM and looks towards the Director and follows his instructions as he says:

Director	The enter'd prentice's sign is given, says Samuel Prichard, by "extending the four fingers of the right hand and drawing of them cross his throat."
Act1	*(Gives the sign, then turns to speak to the Narrator.)* That does not seem right.

Other actors try the sign out for themselves, shaking their heads towards the audience in disagreement.

Narrator	It gets more odd.

Act4, rises, walks up and faces the WM.

WM	Give me the word.
Act4	I'll letter it with you.
WM	B …

Act4 and the WM letter the word together. Act2 then walks up and joins Act4 facing the WM.

WM	Give me another.
Act2	I'll letter it with you.
WM	J …

Act 4 and the WM letter the word together. Both actors return to their places.

Director	But — <u>two words </u>in the <u>same</u> degree?
Narrator	That is what Samuel Prichard wrote.

Director	And the sign is wrong as well?
Narrator	It may well be.
Director	So was there one word for each degree or two?
Narrator	We don't know. Both words occur together in the EA degree in most English exposures before Prichard. Have one of your colleagues give us a section of one of the earliest, from the year 1700.

Act2 walks to the East. Other actors rise and mime the actions in the West while Act2 speaks — deliberately pronouncing the word 'yow' to rhyme with 'cow'.)

Act 2	*Imprima*, yow are to put the person, who is to get the word, upon his knees: And after a great many ceremonies to frighten him, yow make him to take up the Bible; and, laying his right hand upon it, yow are to conjure him to secrecy by threatening that if he shall break his oath, the sun in the firmament and all the company there present will be witnesses against him which will be an occasion of his damnation. And likewise they will be sure to murder him. After he promised secrecy, they give him the oath as follows: The words are J ... & B ...

Actors remain motionless frozen in posture.

Director	Two words again!
Narrator	Yes. The words have caused a lot of trouble.
Director	Are you going to tell us about that?
Narrator	We shall come to it.
Director	I think we need a break for a song.
Narrator	Good idea. Singing played a large part in the meetings of our earlier brethren. Let's have the *Enter'd Prentice's Song*, written by by Bro. Matthew Birkhead.

Actors hand out song sheets to the lodge at large.

Director	Brethren, our musicians will play the tune through once and then we will all join in.

Actors encourage everyone to join in.

> COME, let us prepare,
> We Brothers that are,
> Assembled on merry occasion.

Let's drink, laugh, and sing,
Our Wine has a Spring,
Here's a health to an Accepted MASON.

The World is in pain,
Our Secrets to gain,
And still let them wonder and gaze on.
They ne'er can divine,
The Word or the Sign,
Of a Free and an Accepted MASON.

'Tis This, and 'tis That,
They cannot tell What,
Why so many GREAT MEN of the Nation,
Should Aprons put on,
To make themselves one,
With a Free and an Accepted MASON.

Great KINGS, DUKES, and LORDS,
Have laid by their Swords,
Our Myst'ry to put a good Grace on,
And ne'er been ashamed,
To hear themselves nam'd,
With a Free and an Accepted MASON.

Actors sit.

Director	Tell us about the trouble the words have caused.
Narrator	It all started with that Samuel Prichard.
Director	He's quite a trouble maker, isn't he?
Narrator	Indeed he is. Perhaps one of your colleagues could read from the Minutes of Grand Lodge, 15 December 1730.

Actors gather around as if a Grand Lodge Meeting. Act5 stands at front as if he is WM. Act1 stands at side as if he is the Secretary. Act2 becomes a lectern. Act1 has collected minute book, which he now places on the 'lectern', opens and reads. Lights centre only.

Act1   *(This is nearly all one sentence, so in reading it Act1 runs out of breath a few times.)* The Deputy Grand

	Master took notice of a pamphlet lately published by one Prichard, who pretends to have been made a regular Mason, in violation of the obligation of a Mason which he swears he has broke in order to do hurt to Masonry. Expressing himself with the utmost indignation against both him (styling him an imposter) and of his book as a foolish thing not to be regarded, the Deputy Grand Master, in order to prevent the lodges being imposed upon by false brethren or imposters, proposed till otherwise ordered by the Grand Lodge, that no person whatsoever should be admitted into lodges unless some member of the lodge then present would vouch for such visiting Brother being a regular Mason, and then the member's name to be entered against the visitor's name in the lodge book.
Act5	All those in favour?
All Actors	Aye!

All show hands in usual manner. Act2 does this as well — perhaps some business about trying to vote while also being a lectern.

| Act5 | That proposition has been carried. Brother Secretary. |

The real lodge Secretary stands.

| Sec | Thank you, Very Worshipful Brother Deputy Grand Master. |

Secretary sits as do all actors. Full stage lighting.

| Director | That sounds a very reasonable proposition. |
| Narrator | Yes, it was the beginning of the signature book that we know today. However, some say they did more than this. Ask one of your colleagues to read a passage said to be from *Hiram*, a 1764 exposure. |

Director hands paper to Act6 who moves to the centre and reads.

| Act6 | Formerly it was the Fellow-Craft's, till a pretended discovery of Free-Masonry came out, wrote by Samuel Prichard, which was about three fourths fiction, and the other fourth real; however it made a great confusion among the Masons at that time, and in order to prevent being imposed upon by Cowans or Imposters, there was a general council held, and the Entered Apprentice and |

	Fellow-Craft's words were exchang'd, tho' there are some lodges still retain the old custom.

Director exchanges the paper for a copy of Bernard Jones' book. Act6 puts on mortar board.

Director	So they exchanged the words in the degrees to catch out imposters. That must have caused some trouble. Imagine how this Lodge would have reacted to something like that!
Narrator	Indeed, one shudders to think. Bernard Jones, the great Masonic historian is quite censorious about the decision.
Act6	Grand Lodge made the alteration with the best of intentions but in doing so was guilty of, at least, a profound error of judgement, and in due course paid a heavy price for its mistake. The alteration was regarded by many of its members, and by the whole of the Masons outside its organisation, as a grievous and wholly improper interference with a landmark purporting to date from time immemorial.

Act4 and Act5 rise and face each other. Act5, offers the back of his hand to Act4 who slaps it as if Act5 has been a naughty boy. Both actors return to their seats.

Director	Let us see how it worked. WM, will you open the lodge in the time of 1760?

The opening is carried out by the real officers of the lodge, guided as necessary by the Director. House lights on to enable officers to read. WM puts on a top hat and gives three knocks.

WM	*(To JD)* What is the care of a Mason?
JD	To see that his lodge is tyl'd.
WM	Pray do your duty.

JD goes to the door and knocks. Tyler replies from <u>inside</u> the lodge, having been invited in to witness the entertainment.

JD	Worshipful, the lodge is tyl'd.
WM	The Junior Deacon's place in the lodge?
JD	At the back of the Senior Warden or at his right hand if he permits it.
WM	Your business?

JD	To carry messages from the Senior to the Junior Warden, so that they may be dispersed around the lodge.
WM	*(Still to JD)* The Senior Deacon's place in the lodge?
JD	At the back of the Master, or at his right hand if he permits it.
WM	*(To SD)* Your business here?
SD	To carry all messages from the Master to the Senior Warden.
WM	*(to SD)* The Junior Warden's place in the lodge?
SD	In the South.
WM	*(to JW)* Your business there?
JW	The better to observe the sun at high meridian; to call the men off from work to refreshment and to see that they come on in due time, that the Master may have pleasure and profit thereby.
WM	*(to JW)* The Senior Warden's place in the lodge?
JW	In the West.
WM	*(to SW)* Your business there?
SW	As the sun sets in the West to close the day, so the senior stands in the West to close the lodge, paying the hirelings their wages and dismissing them from labour.
WM	*(to SW)* The Master's place in the lodge?
SW	In the East.
WM	Why is he placed there?
SW	As the sun rises in the East to open the day, so the Master stands in the East to open his lodge to set his men to work.
WM	*(Takes off his hat.)* This lodge is open, in the name of God and holy St John, forbidding all cursing and swearing, whispering, and all profane discourse whatsoever, under the no less penalty than what the majority shall think proper, not less than one penny a time, nor more than six pence.

WM gives three knocks and puts top hat on again. Knocks are echoed by the SW and the JW and by the Tyler — again from inside. Music — an opening ode. No singing — just fade the music under the Narrator as he says ...

Narrator	That was the opening of the lodge from the exposure *Three Distinct Knocks*, published in 1760, some 30 years after Prichard. Let us go on a bit.
Director	*(Rises and moves to centre of lodge)* Brethren, some of you have GREEN cards. Hold them up. Good! Please be ready to read your answer in turn. We start with Green card number 1. Back to you WM.

Actors identify the brethren who have cards. (G1=Green card 1)

WM	After you had received your obligation, what was the first thing that was said to you?
Brother G1	I was asked what I most desir'd.
WM	What was your answer?
Brother G2	To be brought to light.
WM	Who brought you to light?
Brother G3	The Master and the rest of the brethren.
WM	After you had been instructed in the greater and lesser lights, what was then done to you?
Brother G4	The Master took me by the right hand and gave me the grip and word of an enter'd apprentice and said, rise up Brother B_____ .
WM	Have you got this grip and word, Brother?
Brother G5	I have, Worshipful.

The Director motions Brother G5 to step forward.

WM	Give it to your next Brother.
Narrator	*(House lights out.)*
	Before you do my Brother, you had better know how the grip was supposed to have been given — by pinching your thumb-nail on your Brother's r h.

Brother G5 gives the grip to the Director and then sits. The Director, in East, turns and gives the grip in turn to Act1.

Act1	What's this?
Director	The grip of an Enter'd Apprentice.
Act1	Has it got a name?
Director	It has.
Act1	Will you give it to me?

99

Director	I'll letter it with you, or halve it.
Act1	I'll halve it with you.
Director	Begin.
Act1	No, you begin first.
Director	*First syllable of B.*
Act1	*Second syllable of B.*

The rest of the actors rise and all form a line in the middle of the lodge. Act1, in dumb show, gives grip to Act2, who turns and so on down the line. At the end of the line, Act6 receives the grip and turns to the WM. Party music as if the actors are playing 'pass the parcel.' Actors crouch so that Act6 can see the WM over them.

Act6	It is right, WM.

Music stops. Actors 6, 2 & 5 stand line abreast in the West. Others actors sit.

Director	Wait a minute. Wait a minute. Wait a minute. I thought you said that the words were changed around in the 1730's. *Three Distinct Knocks*, you tell us, was published in 1760 but the word B ___ is still there.
Narrator	You are right but *Three Distinct Knocks* reflects the practice of the premier Grand Lodge, the one that is said to have changed the words.
Director	There was more than one Grand Lodge?
Narrator	Yes, the premier Grand Lodge was founded in 1717 but in 1751, another Grand Lodge appeared: the Grand Lodge of the Antients. They maintained they alone kept the original landmarks and caused a split in Masonry lasting more than 50 years. Take a look at the words in another exposure, *Shibboleth* published in 1765.
Act6	Formerly Masons, upon admittance of a new member, used a prayer which the MODERNS omit, and as soon as the oath is taken, proceed to teach the signs, grip and password of an entered apprentice as follows:
Act2	The sign is given by drawing your right hand across your throat edgeways, indicating that an entered apprentice would sooner have his throat cut than reveal the secrets of the Craft.

All actors rise and give sign facing outwards to the audience.

Act5	The grip is taking a Brother with your r h and pressing hard with your thumb nail upon his h. The word is whispering in his ear J ...

Act5 gives this grip to Act2 whispering the word who gives it to Act6 speaking a little louder. Director eavesdrops.

Director	*(Turns to Narrator.)* Ah-ha! J ... ! The word has been changed.
Narrator	Not so fast! *Shibboleth* describes the workings of the Antients Grand Lodge who claimed to have maintained the original landmarks.
Act1	*(musingly)* ... with the words in the right order?
Act4	So the words today are in the *wrong* order?
Act2	So J ... is the *real* EA word *(chord)*
Act5	and B ... is *really* the *FC* word? *(chord)*
Narrator	Well it seems possible, doesn't it?
Director	Is there any more evidence?
Narrator	Let us take a trip to France where Freemasonry was very different. In England, Scotland and Ireland, most Masons were middle class people but in France, early Freemasonry was for the aristocracy.

18th century French music. The actors stand up, put on sashes, hats and swords. The actors parade around the lodge in a showy sort of way. Music stops.

Director	What exposure are we looking at now?
Narrator	One written by L'Abbé Gabriel Louis Calabre Perau in 1742, entitled *Le Secret des Francs-Macons*.
Director	*The Secret of the Freemasons*?
Narrator	That's right.

The actors mime the ceremony. The Director directs the dumb show. Music very quietly under the voice.

> The lodge of initiation should consist of several rooms, one of which must be in total darkness.

Lights out except West.

> It is to this room that the sponsor brings the candidate. They ask him if he feels the necessary desire to be received; he replies:

Act4 *(as candidate)* Oui.

Actors mime applause for Candidate's command of French. Candidate bows & gives thumbs up. During what follows, actors set up the lodge in West with floor covering and candles. Candles in centre are lit.

Narrator   Then he is deprived of all metal articles such as buckles, buttons, rings, snuff-boxes, etc. There are some lodges where they carry correctness so far as to deprive a man of his clothes if they are ornamented with metal braid. After this, they lay bare his right knee and make him wear his left shoe as a slipper.

Then they put a bandage over his eyes and he is left to his own reflections for about an hour; the room in which he waits is guarded inside and out by Brother Wardens with drawn swords in hand. The sponsor waits with the candidate but does not speak.

The sponsor strikes three times upon the door of the initiation room. *(Tyler knocks three times from inside.)* The Worshipful Grand Master *(WM knocks)* responds from within by three other knocks and orders the door to be opened, that the candidate be allowed to enter in; the Wardens place themselves either side, to conduct him.

Two actor wardens do so.

In the centre of the lodge room is a large space on which are drawn two columns, relics of the temple of Solomon; on either side of this space are drawn a capital J and a capital B. In the centre of the space, there are three lighted candles, arranged in the form of a triangle.

Actors lay out a sheet with the Lodge drawn on it, place the candles in position and take the candidate around three times.

The candidate is led three times round, and then to the centre of the space where he is made to advance by three steps towards the Worshipful and the Gospel according to St John.

IPM hurriedly changes the pages of the VSL, the implication being that it was open at the Old Testament as usual. Music stops.

Director   The Grand Master then asks the candidate:

WM	(*Uses 'Ello 'Ello comic French accent throughout this section.*) Do you feel zee vocation to be received?
Act4	(*as candidate*) Oui.
WM	Let him see zee day. He 'as been deprived of zee light long enough.
Narrator	The brethren then remove the bandage from his eyes and while doing this, they form a circle round him, with drawn swords in their hands, all pointed towards him. (*Actors do so.*) The candidate is then advanced three steps to a stool which stands at the foot of the armchair and on which are displayed a square and compasses. A brother, called the orator, then says:
WM	You are about to enter zee order most respectable, which is much more serious than you may imagine. It admits of nossing contrary to zee law of religion or zee king nor anything contrary to zee morals.
Director	The candidate is told to rest his knee on the stool and the Worshipful Grand Master says to him:

Act4 kneels in front of the WM.

WM	(*still using the accent*) Do you promise nevair to delineate, to write, nor to reveal zee secrets of Free-Masons & of Masonry except to a brozzair inside zee lodge and in zee presence of the Worshipful Grand Mastair?[53]
Act4	Oui.
Narrator	They next uncover his breast to see that it is not a woman who has presented herself; and although there are some women who are hardly better than men in this respect, they are good enough to be satisfied with a cursory examination.
Director	Are you reading from the text?
Narrator	Oui — I mean yes. That is what the Abbé wrote! Next they place the point of the compasses to the candidate's left breast. The candidate holds it in his left hand, lays his right hand upon the Gospel and pronounces the oath.
Director	Is the oath different from that we have already heard?

---

[53] Listening to Hercule Poirot will give you a feel for *Franglais* word order.

Narrator	Not really.
Director	We'll skip that then. What next?
Narrator	When the oath is ended, the candidate kisses the Gospel and the brethren give him the Freemason's apron. They also give him a pair of gloves for himself and a pair of lady's gloves for the Lady he esteems most. This lady may be the candidate's wife or belong to him in some other fashion. They do not worry much about this point. *(Actors freeze.)*
Director	Are you sure you are reading from the text?
Narrator	Yes, yes! But listen to this. Then they instruct the newly-made Mason in the signs and explain the meaning of the letters drawn in the space on the floor — that is to say:

Actors positioned around floor cloth, point down at the letter J.

Act2	The letter J, which represents the word J ... *(chord)*
All	J ... ?
Director	J ... So maybe the original word *was* J ...

Full stage lights on quickly.

Narrator	Virtually all French exposures use J ... What may be further evidence for this comes from the plagiarism that we spoke of earlier. This exposure, *Le secret des Francs-Macons* was copied word for word into another exposure ...
Act2	*L'Ordre des Francs-Macons Trahi* — or the *Order of the Freemasons Betrayed* to translate its title ...
Act1	which also has the word J ...
Narrator	which was pirated by another rogue into English as ...
Act4	*A Master Key to Freemasonry*
Narrator	which in its turn was stolen by an exposure published in 1762 as ...
Act5	*J... and B ...* in that order.
Narrator	the rest of which was stolen from the 1760 exposure ...
Act6	*Three Distinct Knocks*
Director	... by which time the EA word has become B ... *(chord)* So we can see the word has changed!

Narrator	Yes, it would seem that J … was the original EA word and that the premier Grand Lodge changed it to B …

Actors make exaggerated faces of amazement at the audience, shake heads in disgust then turn and return to their seats.

Director	The problem is whether you can rely upon such a bunch of rogues and rascals who stole most of their work from other writers, while pretending to be exposing the rituals of Freemasonry.
Narrator	Exactly.
Director	So Stephen Knight is nothing new — just one of many rogues who sought to make money by exposing and attacking Freemasonry?
Narrator	Not that what he had to say was original. The first attack on Freemasonry that I know of, was published in 1698.

Music — Actors move around the lodge quickly as if on their way to somewhere in a hurry. Set up soap box. Lots of business and movement. Actors hand out placards to brethren. Actors encourage brethren to shout slogans. Lots of noise.

Act4	*(Calls out loudly)* Hear me! Hear me!

Actors rush about and get some of the brethren to join them shouting on the 'stage'. Music very loud. If possible, the musicians also move about amongst the crowd. They might be busking and some of the actors can give them a coin or two.

Act4	Hear me! Hear me!

Act 4 stands on soap box. Act1 becomes his assistant and starts to hand out leaflets to the other actors and brethren in the lodge. Still lots of noise. Actors gather around the soap box and get those brethren on stage to do so as well — but still lots of noise.

Act4	Hear me! (*Uses narrator's microphone*) Hear me!

Music quietens, noise subsides. Actors get brethren to sit down again. Lights focus on soap box.

Act4	All Godly people, in the City of London! Hear me!

Quiet descends. Music stops.

Act4	Having thought it needful to warn you of the mischiefs and evils practised in the sight of God by those called Freemasons, I say take care lest their ceremonies and

	secret swearings take hold of you — and be wary that none cause you to err from Godliness.
Actors	Oooh!

Act2 pushes Act4 off the soap box and climbs up himself and continues. Threatening music starts.

Act2	For this devilish sect of men are meeters in secret which swear against all without their following. They are the anti-Christ which was to come leading men from fear of God. For how should men meet in secret places and with secret signs taking care that none observe them to do the work of God; are not these the ways of evil-doers?
Actors	Aaah! *(Music pauses)*

Act1 pushes Act4 off the soap box. Music starts again.

Act1	Knowing how that God observeth privily them that sit in darkness, they shall be smitten and the secrets of their hearts layed bare. Mingle not among this corrupt people lest you be found so at the world's conflagration.

Music reaches crescendo.

Actors	Oooh! *(Music stops)*
Act6	*(Calls out to Act1)* How do y<u>ou</u> know?*)*
Act1	Well - er - I don't!
Actors	Oh!

All actors freeze. Full stage lighting.

Director	I think that sums it up, don't you?
Narrator	Indeed I do.

Music — a jolly 'catch'. Actors line up facing the East and bow to the WM. They bow to the South, the West and North. The Director gets the WM to rise and take a bow. The Director waves to the officers of the lodge who stand and bow. Music stops. The Director brings forward the musicians for a bow. Actors exit.

ಐ ಐ ಐ

The 'truth' about the words

Tell the truth. Tell me who's been fooling you?
Tell the truth. Who's been fooling who?

Bobby Whitlock, Eric Clapton, Eric Patrick Clapton. Sung by Eric Clapton

Exposure! was written as an entertainment to stimulate critical thinking about the history of our ritual and the exposures, ancient and modern. We used the word *shocking* in our advertisements, as did the adverts for Stephen Knight's book, to show how that word is misused but, unlike Knight's stuff, there is something behind our shock horror.

It is the established theory that Grand Lodge changed the word for the first degree to J, August 28 1730, on a proposition by Dr Desaguliers, reacting to the publication of *Masonry Dissected* and that they changed it back again to B sometime around 1770. While the Grand Lodge minutes mention the introduction of what became our signature book, there is no mention of a change in the words. Here is a list of English and Scottish exposures with their first degree words:

1. c1700 *Chetwode Crawley* — Two words, J then B
2. c1700 *Sloane* — J then B
3. c1710 *Dumfries* — J then B
4. c1714 *Kevan* — J then B
5. 1723 *A Mason's Examination* — J then B

6. 1724 *Grand Mystery of Freemasons Disc'd* — G (Inst M's word) then B
7. 1724 *Whole Institution of Masonry* — J
8. 1725 *Institution of Free Masons* — Probably G then another word erased

9. 1727 *A Mason's Confession* — B
10. 1727 *Wilkinson* — B
11. 1730 *The Mystery of Freemasonry* — B
12. 1730 *Masonry Dissected* — Two words, B then J
13. 1740 *Dialogue between Simon and Philip* — B
14. 1760 *Three Distinct Knocks* — B

15. 1761 *Hiram* — J
16. 1762 *J & B* — B
17. 1765 *Shibboleth* — J

From 1 to 5 in the list, the use of two words, with J first and B second, is unanimous. There is something of a mixture from 6 to 8 with the temporary appearance of a third word. From 9 to 14, B predominates although 12, Prichard's *Masonry Dissected*, goes back to two words but in reverse order. About 1760, something else seems to occur and two of the three exposures use J on its own.

We do not have to accept that the writers of exposures were always accurate or up to the minute in their reporting. Changes were clearly occurring in the ritual[54] and the exposures made guesses at them; sometimes getting things right, frequently getting things wrong and very frequently getting things partly right and partly wrong. In seeking to follow the development of the ritual, we have little else to go on but the use of a large pinch of salt is recommended.

So, taking our pinch, it seems it was normal at first to use two words, J then B, but in about 1724, something caused a change. This something was a matter of uncertainty and the reporting of the change is somewhat stuttering. A new word gets reported and then disappears again. Eventually, one word, B, wins out as the EA word, although J makes a bit of a come back later.

It is interesting to note that Prichard, far from being the cause of these changes, is actually behind the times; still reporting the use of two words in 1730, albeit in a reverse order, when the use of one word has become normal. What is more, the change from two to one word — that word being B — occurs at least three years before the publication of Prichard's book. So if the Premier Grand Lodge issued an edict about the words, they did not do so in response to Prichard's book.

I think we see here something far more interesting than a reaction to an exposure: a sort of audit trail of the development of the three degrees.

Phase One — to about 1720 + or - a couple of years

There is only one degree, that of initiation. J and B are both used.

Phase Two — from about 1720 to about 1724

The second degree is born, and the two words previously used together are separated, one word for each degree. During this phase, there is confusion and many lodges are uncertain about the new degree and how

---

[54] They always have been and still are. See T. O. Haunch, *It is not in the power of any man: a study in change*, 1972 Prestonian Lecture in *The Collected Prestonian Lectures, Volume Two, 1961-1974*, Lewis Masonic 1983.

to use the words. Interestingly, the G word appears fleetingly, quite possibly indicating the initial birth pangs of the third degree.

Phase Three — from about 1726 to about 1760

One word becomes established as the EA word. It might have seemed logical for lodges to use J as the EA word and B for the new FC degree, given the original J & B order. However something happens to prevent this — which may well have been a pronouncement from the Premier Grand Lodge, made to counter the irregular making of masons. During this phase, *Masonry Dissected* is published, trying to be up to date but getting things only partially right. It puts B first, perhaps catching wind of a change that has been made, but wrongly includes J as well.

Phase Four — from 1751 until the Union.

(a) The Ancients

Perhaps adopting the logic of the original J & B order, the Grand Lodge of the Antients is formed and uses J for the first degree and B for the second. How do we know this?

It is the accepted view that the Antients Grand Lodge stemmed from Irish Masons emigrating to England. In *Three Distinct Knocks (TDK)*, which uses B, there is a vicious attack on Irishmen. *Shibboleth*, using J, is known only in three editions, two of which are Irish. *Hiram*, also using J, ran to three editions in Ireland of which the third (a facsimile of which I am using) had three reprints. So it seems logical to assume that *Shibboleth* and *Hiram* expose Antients' ritual, with J as the EA word, while *TDK* exposes the Premier Grand Lodge ritual, using B.

(b) French usage

Here are exposures that give us information on the EA word used:

1. 1737 *Réception d'un Frey-Maçon*   J then B
2. 1738 *La Réception Mysterieuse*   B then J
3. 1742 *Le Secret des Francs-Maçons*   J
4. 1745 *Le Sceau Rompu*   No EA word but FC is J
5. 1745 *L'Ordre des Francs-Maçons Trahi*   J
6. 1747 *La Désolation des Entrepreneurs Modernes* J
7. 1748 *L'Anti-Maçon*   J
8. 1751 *Le Maçon Demasqué*   J

It is said that French Freemasonry[55] was derived from English Masonry, sometime between 1726 and 1736. It is interesting to note that *Réception d'un Frey-Maçon* (1), fits in with English exposures up to 1723 and that *La Réception Mysterieuse* (2) uses two words in the same order as Prichard. Indeed, *La Réception Mysterieuse* pretends that Prichard has written it.

Le Secret des Francs-Maçons (3) is the exposure written by L'Abbé Perau and uses one word, J for the EA. This antedates the Grand Lodge of the Antients and seems to indicate that French lodges use J for the EA as soon as the second degree appears. It is clear that French go on using J as the EA word, despite any change in England and, I am told by a distinguished member of the *Grande Loge National Française,* many French lodges still use J today. If there was a change in England, it did not affect French Freemasonry nor the later Grand Lodge of the Antients. The PGL was unique in using B for the first degree at a time when the Antients and the French were using J.

Phase Five — around 1813

So, if the PGL did change the words, the change was from J to B. The established theory holds that the Premier Grand Lodge reversed its edict in or around 1770 but that is obviously false. It would imply that the PGL switched (back) from B to J but it has been B all the way.

The fifth phase[56] is wrapped up in the discussions and negotiations that led to the union of the two Grand Lodges. That must have been some discussion! Somehow, the Antients accepted a fundamental change in the words of an EA and an FC. How fundamental would that have been? Well, Bernard E Jones writes[57] that the Moderns (the Premier Grand Lodge) were charged by the Antients with having transposed the modes of recognition in the first and second degrees. He says that the Antients regarded this as an alteration of a landmark, *something quite impossible to be countenanced.*

---

[55] This list is taken from From *The Early French Exposures*, edited by Harry Carr, *Quatuor Coronati* Lodge, No 2076, 1971.

[56] One would like to say that there is an earlier fifth phase in 1766 with the word *J...h* appearing. Sadly this is not the first signs of the RA but almost certainly an exposer getting it wrong. After all, the original RA word was *J...n* and *J...h* was substituted by edict of the Grand Chapter, an edict that we do have evidence for.

[57] *Freemasons' Guide and Compendium*, Bernard E. Jones, Harrap, 1950.

Commentators have said the Antients won most of the arguments. After all, we have Deacons, an esoteric installation ceremony and the Royal Arch — all of which the Antients wanted and the Premier Grand Lodge didn't. Perhaps that was the deal for accepting the PGL's EA word! A cover up? Well, enough evidence to create an exposure!

ಙ ಙ ಙ

Old Masters (l to r) from 1992, 1993 and 1991 respectively

A White Table

> *When she catches up with me*
> *Won't be no time to explain*
> *She thinks I've been with another woman*
> *And that's enough to send her half insane*
> *Gonna buy a fast car*
> *Put on my lead boots*
> *And take a long, long drive*
> *I may end up spending all my money*
> *But I'll still be alive*
> Jon Entwhistle. Sung by The Who.

A *White Table*[58] is an event to which ladies and other non-Masonic guests are invited in order to view the lodge and dine with the brethren. During such an event, we take the time to explain what we do — no need of lead boots and a long, long drive!

It is a major undertaking for any lodge but if a lodge is short of things to do, it may well find the time. The management of a White Table involves a large number of brethren which is all to the good and its success gives everyone a lift. To give you some ideas, I will describe a process that has been used by our lodge. Obviously, you will find many points at which you have to diverge from it to fit your own needs and circumstances, but I hope it will prove a useful spark to your creativity.

Why a White Table?

While non-masons who attend may well express interest in becoming Freemasons, in our experience a White Table is best for:

- showing our ladies what we get up to on lodge nights.
- providing some positive publicity concerning the lodge in particular and Masonry in general.
- enabling non-Masons to understand the values of Masonry.
- persuading people in the local public eye that Masonry is a force for good.

---

[58] I suppose the derivation of the name is that while our earlier brethren dined off bare boards, a table cloth was used when ladies were present. Possible anyway.

- influencing people who might in turn influence candidates in the future.
- involving a large number of members and bringing about even greater closeness and lodge spirit.
- and making the lodge feel good about itself.

In other words, the benefits are real but indirect.

The purposes of the event dictate the guest list. For example, if a lodge hopes to provide positive publicity and to persuade local opinion that the lodge is a force for good, then it may seek the attendance of local media (the press, radio and TV) and of the Mayor, the local MP, members of the local Council, the head teachers of local schools and so on.[59] If these people accept, the lodge needs a plan to manage their attendance: to make them feel welcome, to answer their questions, provide photo opportunities and so on. You want person to person management — like man to man marking in earlier football days. The table plan also needs careful handling (but do not be surprised or concerned if such guests leave early. While we see the evening as enjoyment, they see it as work.)

The media

The press want a story; so you must prepare one for them. For example, tell them about your own (local) charitable giving and try to get a figure for the total charity giving per year from your Masonic centre; perhaps, identify some recent attacks and have a clear story on why they are false; or prepare an analysis of the sort of people who become Freemasons by analysing your membership.

Never give an opinion on what you don't know about but do give information that the journalist can use. If you do not provide a story, the journalist may make one up — and existing prejudices and stereotypes are all too easy a basis to work on. Have the information ready for him/her in print or, better still, on a memory stick. The typical free newspaper has one overworked journalist who will really appreciate help in getting a story into print.

Talk to the brother who handles regional or provincial PR and media matters. Invite him along to the meeting, with his lady. One of our

---

[59] Our local MP attended our 2000 White Table as did two Councillors, all with their ladies. None were Freemasons. They all said that they enjoyed the event, understood more about our order and appreciated that it was a force for good.

brethren was responsible for PR in a multinational and you may find that one of your brethren has similar experience.

Our purpose

Our aim was to describe to our ladies as fully as possible what we did as Masons and to show that Masonry has a higher purpose than dressing up to eat and drink too much. We also wanted to deliver that message outside our own families and to gain some positive publicity. We wanted to do something big in order to show the lodge could (still) do it.

We decided to invite both ladies and male non-masonic guests. In the event, a number of masonic guests also attended, in many cases bringing their ladies with them. Some brother masons from other lodges attended together with candidates for their own lodges. We anticipated that we could handle no more than 110 people dining in our hall although a number of factors reduced this to a more manageable 96 on the day. A rule of thumb for any big event is that around 10% of attendees will drop out at the last minute.

Printing

We printed invitation cards and a colour brochure about our lodge and Masonry in general. We prepared a welcome pack for each guest which included a pictorial quiz[60] based on famous Freemasons, to occupy our audience during any *longeurs*.

Equipment

We used a laptop pc, a powerful projector linked to it, a very, very large screen and a podium. We rehearsed with the equipment two or three times to ensure that we could set it up quickly and to accustom brethren to its use. This meant hire fees but we thought the investment worthwhile. We discovered exactly how the lights in the temple were controlled and planned the lighting at every point. We did not use a sound system but probably should have done so. We have now bought our own and use it often.

Rehearsals

Although most of the words were to be read, we still rehearsed. Reading aloud to an audience is not as easy as it seems and it is also important to manage the transitions from one speaker to the next. Much time can be

---

[60] Take a look at at http://stlaurencelodge.org.uk/masonic-quiz/.

lost in clumsy handovers and the audience can become fidgety. So unlike many British sprint relay teams, we practised! Few brethren had learned to project their voice and practice was essential for this as well. Several speakers wanted to make changes to their script to fit their own style — which was right and proper. The organist was asked to prepare music for the event.

Formal lodge meeting

Although a White Table can be held on a day other than the regular lodge meeting date, we decided to hold a brief lodge meeting beforehand. This, we felt, increased the ambience enabling guests to feel they were genuinely entering a temple set out for a lodge meeting.

Our usual meeting time is 3.15 pm on a Saturday and this served our purposes admirably. The brethren were asked to arrive at least ten minutes before the lodge was to be opened and to clothe inside the temple so that their regalia was not on display before the event. This was purely for dramatic reasons. The brethren signed in at the Secretary's table instead of the more usual Tyler's table outside the door of the lodge. All brethren were told that latecomers could not be admitted to the formal lodge meeting as time was precious. In the event, three brethren did turn up late and were not admitted. The Master drove the meeting along at a brisk pace and closed it at 4.00 pm.

Guests arrive

Meanwhile, all non-masonic guests arrived and were entertained to tea and cakes. They were asked to sign against a pre-printed list of guests. The temple seating plan was explained to everyone and guests introduced to each other by a number of brethren who stayed outside the meeting proper (including the late comers!)

Processions out and in

At the end of the formal lodge meeting, brethren stood by their seats while the Master and his Wardens processed out as normal. Guests were then invited to enter the temple and take their assigned seats next to their hosts. The Master with his lady, accompanied by his Wardens and their ladies, then entered in procession in a manner as close as possible to the normal procession. From this moment on, brethren were to give no salutes, nor use any Masonic words or signs. If a Brother felt his hand and arm going into a salute as a reflex action, he was to turn the movement into the Sign of Reverence! We included a quasi-formal procession to welcome one of our own brethren who happens to be Past Deputy Provincial Grand Master of Flandres, GLNF. It enabled us to demonstrate such a procession and talk about Masonry universal.

Seating

The temple was near to its capacity and we found a seating plan vital for the meeting as well as for the Festive Board. This meant some unusual seating arrangements for the formal lodge meeting beforehand as the plan was designed to accommodate the guests who would enter later. As usual we had what we call 'the blue corner' where we seated Grand Officers with their ladies, together with two ladies who were Grand Officers in women's Freemasonry. On the Master's left we sat the IPM as usual with his lady but also the Master's lady, the father of the lodge and his lady and an East End prompter – a brother with delegated responsibility for managing unscheduled events in the East. (There was an equivalent in the West.)

All officers sat in their normal chairs but with their ladies beside them. Since we erected the projector screen in front of the Senior Warden's pedestal, we had pre-arranged seats to which to move the Senior Warden, Junior Deacon and Inner Guard with their ladies. The lectern was next to the screen in the south-west and speakers were urged to start moving towards it immediately they were introduced.

The PC and projector were set up on a table in the centre of the lodge and this, together with the setting up of the screen, necessitated a short break. In the event, this lasted no more than four or five minutes and guests were highly entertained by the brethren's attempt to prevent the screen from destroying a chandelier.

The script

We used a variety of media to keep the interest alive; talks illustrated by slides, music, humour, some ritual from memory and audience participation.

With two exceptions, nothing in the script was ritual. The exceptions were an excerpt from the *Charge to the Initiate* and the *Long Closing*. Both of these were carried out from memory. The rest was read. (I have included our full script below in case it helps.) Speakers were told not to look at their slides while speaking but continue with their talk willy-nilly. It was the slide operator's task to ensure the right slide at the right moment and he was assisted by a slide checker who double-checked that the slide showing was the correct one.

Final procession

The final procession included the Master and his Wardens accompanied by their ladies, and all Grand Officers and their ladies. To prevent an unseemly rush to the bar, free drinks awaited, already poured, in the ante-room. In the event, the White Table took just over the hour and everyone had left the temple by 5.30 pm.

Festive Board

Brethren and guests were seated, again according to a table plan. The DC called the room to order and the Master and his lady entered. The Master gavelled; grace was given and dinner served. The menu was chosen to be acceptable to ladies, rather lighter than the school dinners usually appreciated by Masons. Special place cards had been designed and printed for the Festive Board. The Master took wine only twice: firstly with his Wardens and their Ladies and secondly with everyone, he and his lady standing while everyone else remained seated. During after dinner coffee, we were entertained for some 20 minutes by a soprano, tenor and pianist from Charles Court Opera — *Arias of Fun*.

Toasts were restricted to HM the Queen, the Grand Master, the Provincial Grand Master, the Master (no speech but a response from the Master) and the visitors (a short speech with a response from a guest.) Brethren had been reminded that there should be no fire but it is remarkable how habits are triggered by events. Still, although the occasional finger was made ready in mid-air, nothing untoward occurred. A raffle made a satisfactory amount for charity and the evening came to a close at 9.45 pm.

The Festive Board seen from the Secretary's viewpoint.

White Table Script

Adapt this script to fit your own purposes and situation. It is not ritual!

Once everyone is seated, the ADC says:

ADC Ladies, gentlemen and brethren. Please receive the Worshipful Master, his Wardens and their Ladies.

Everyone stands. The WM and his Wardens with their Ladies at their side and preceded by the Deacons and the ADC (whose ladies will be standing by their seats in lodge) enter the Lodge in procession. When everyone is in place, the ADC says:

ADC Please be seated.

All sit. The WM gavels and is answered by the Wardens.

Master Ladies and gentlemen. Welcome to this the … Lodge number … on the register of the Grand Lodge of … Thankyou for coming today and I hope that you will enjoy the meeting this afternoon and the Festive Board which will follow.

 Our aim today is to give you some insight into what it is to be a Freemason; what it means to us. You may think that Freemasonry is about men-as-boys running around in funny clothes and calling each other funny names. There is some truth in that but if it were nothing more, Freemasonry would not have lasted the 300 years or so that it has since the formation of the first Grand Lodge in 1717.

 If you asked the brethren what they get out of membership, they would say many different things. However, most would point to fellowship and mutual support, a feeling of doing the right things, a sense of continuity with the past and future, the satisfaction of ritual well performed, perhaps an enjoyment of the theatre aspects, a great deal of laughter, a few drinks, a good meal … and something not easy to put into words.

 While many of the brethren might be a little embarrassed to say it out loud, what we really gain is a feeling of something beyond ourselves, something that lifts us onto a higher plane, that makes us want to live up to the ideals of Freemasonry.

 Today, we'd like you to catch a glimpse of this and so we will show you some of the ritual and its moral teaching. Most of what we show you will not be actual ritual but something like it. However, we will give you two genuine extracts.

	In all our meetings, we go through a procedure known as opening the lodge so now I will use something like it to introduce our progressive officers, those on their way to this chair. (*Gavels*) Bro. Inner Guard. (*IG steps to the edge of the pavement.*) Please tell us who you are and what you do. (*Officers speak from memory.*)
IG	I guard the door on the inside and ensure that only members and candidates are allowed to enter.
Master	Brother JD.
JD	I guide the candidates round the Lodge during the ceremony of initiation and help the Senior Deacon at other times.
Master	Brother SD.
SD	I guide the candidates during the higher ceremonies and help the Junior Deacon as required. The Junior Deacon and I are involved in the voting process and the collection of alms.
Master	Brother JW.
JW	I mark the sun at midday. I am responsible for visitors.
Master	Brother SW.
SW	I mark the setting sun. I close the Lodge, when every Brother has had his due.
Master	Brother IPM. The Master?
IPM	The Master sits in the East to open his Lodge and employ the brethren in Freemasonry.
Master	So ladies and gentlemen, my name is … and I am Master for this year. A new Master is installed each year and next year the Senior Warden will take over from me. Now, having, so to speak, opened the Lodge, I call upon our Secretary, Brother … to explain the proceedings.
Secretary	Ladies and gentlemen. We thought you'd like to know a bit about the ritual, a bit about the history, something about the origins of the Lodge, what it all costs, something about Masonic charity and something about the place of women in Freemasonry. (*IG goes to the door and opens it a crack. He ensures that the Tyler is ready. Waits there to give Tyler the cue for 4 knocks.*) We have organised some short illustrated talks and of course we welcome your questions. I now call upon our Chaplain, the officer who leads all prayers in the lodge, who will tell you a little * about our ritual.

*At * IG cues the Tyler for **four loud** knocks on door.*

IG	Steps to pavement. *No salute.* Bro. JW. There is a report.
JW	WM. There is a report.
Master	Bro. JW. Enquire who wants admission.
JW	Bro. IG. See who seeks admission.

IG opens door and is given a card. He returns to the pedestal and reads:

IG	WM. W. Bro. AB Past Provincial Senior Grand Deacon in the Province of Essex and Holder of London Grand Rank is outside the door of your Lodge and *requests* admission.
Master	Admit him Bro. IG.

IG goes to the door and lets AB in. AB steps to edge of pavement.

AB	WM. Very Worshipful Brother CD, Past Deputy Provincial Grand Master of the Province of Flanders in the *Grande Loge Nationale Française*, is outside the door of your Lodge and *desires* admission.
Master	We will admit him with pleasure. (*Gavels*).
AB	WM. Have I your permission to form a column to welcome the Past Deputy Provincial Grand Master in to your Lodge?
Master	You have.
AB	(*Calls upon selected brethren.*) Brethren, please form up in the North West of the Lodge.

Selected brethren form a column of two lines. IG opens door and each line faces inwards towards the other. The Deacons raise wands to form arch and the distinguished guest moves along the line, through the arch to shake hands with the WM. AB then says:

AB	Be seated brethren.

The column disperses and everyone sits. AB takes his seat in the NE. Chaplain steps forward in the SW to the podium.

Slide 1 (*Lodge emblem*)

Chaplain Ladies and gentlemen. What just happened demonstrates a couple of things about us. One is that we do like a bit of ceremony! Another is that Freemasonry is international. Brother CD is a member of this Lodge and also of *Le Touquet Lodge* in France. There are Grand Lodges more or less all over the world – from Iceland to India and from Brazil to Bosnia.

In France, Bro. CD is a Past Deputy Provincial Grand Master – a rather important rank. When someone with such a rank visits a lodge, we receive him as you have just seen. We know just how much Bro CD puts into Freemasonry and the ceremony recognises this.

Slide 2 *(Collar jewel)*

The rank that a Brother holds is shown partly by his apron and badge and partly by his collar and jewel. My apron is dark blue and I am a Provincial Grand Officer. My actual rank is Past Provincial … Something of a mouthful, I agree! Bro. EF, *(He stands)* over there, is Past Provincial … The badge on his apron and the jewel on his collar are different.

Over in the 'Blue Corner' we keep some very special exhibits – the Grand Officers. You can recognise them by their highly decorated collars and aprons. *(Each stand in order)* Bro. GH is Assistant Provincial Grand Master. You can call him John. We tend to call him sir! We also have with us Bro. IJ, Bro. KL, and Bro. MN. Welcome, brethren all.

So let's get back to ritual matters. We work an age old ritual; much of it telling a story, a form of teaching and learning that predates books. It reminds us of the virtues we should practise. Freemasonry is a peculiar system of morality, veiled in allegory and illustrated by symbols. Everything in the Lodge serves to inculcate the principles of piety and virtue.

Slide 3 *(Mosaic pavement)*

For example, take the floor of the Lodge – which we refer to as the mosaic pavement. It reminds us of the uncertainty of all things. Bro. OP.

Brother OP stands and reads:

As the steps of man are trod in the various and uncertain incidents of life, so are his days variegated and chequered by a strange contrariety of events. Today we may travel in prosperity; tomorrow we may totter on the uneven path of weakness, temptation, and adversity. So with this emblem before us, we are instructed to walk uprightly and with humility before God, there being no station in life on which pride can with stability be founded. While our feet tread on this mosaic, we hope, as good men and Freemasons, to live in harmony, unity and brotherly love.

Brother OP sits. Chaplain continues:

Slide 4 *(Working tools)*

> The gavel, the rule, the square, the compasses, the plumb-line, the level and the trowel are tools used by the operative stone mason. As Freemasons we do not build in stone but in virtue and so we apply these tools to morals. Bro. QR.

Brother QR stands and reads:

> Let every Mason beat down any evil disposition with the gavel of righteousness and measure out his actions by the rule of one day. Let him fit them to the square of prudence and equity; keep them within the bounds of the compass of moderation; adjust them by the true plumb-line of sincerity and the just level of perfection and spread them abroad with the silent trowel of peace and charity.

Brother QR sits. Chaplain continues:

> Our actual ritual we learn by heart. Our teacher is known as our Preceptor.

Slide 5 *(Ritual book)*

Precep If you commute by bus or train, you may see a man apparently talking to himself, looking up in the air, sighing and looking down at a small book. No, he is not a literary critic or a schoolmaster reading a pupil's essay. He is a Mason, learning the ritual, repeating it to himself, getting stuck and taking a peek at the book.

We rehearse the ritual at our weekly Lodge of Instruction under the strict eye of a severe headmaster known as the Preceptor. I am the Preceptor of this Lodge! I am very severe!

I will now ask Bro. ST to give you, from memory, part of what we call the *Charge to the Initiate*. This is a genuine extract from our ritual. I want you to imagine that Bro. ST is talking to a Brother who has just been initiated.

Actually, let us do it properly. We will borrow one of our guests here today to stand in as the initiate. Mr UV – would you assist? *(ADC guides Mr UV to the NE, facing South.)* Brother Deacons. Please assist.

Deacons square the lodge, to stand each side of Mr UV. Bro ST moves to the SE, facing N.

Slide 6 *(An initiate)*

ST Having passed through the ceremony of your initiation, I congratulate you on being admitted a member of our ancient and honourable Institution. Ancient no doubt it is having subsisted from time immemorial and honourable it must be acknowledged to be as by a natural tendency it conduces to make all those so who are obedient to its precepts. Indeed no institution can boast a more solid foundation that that on which Freemasonry rests, the practice of every moral and social virtue; and to so high an eminence has its credit been advanced that in every age Monarchs …

***Slide 7** (Royal Freemasons)*

… themselves have been promoters of the art, have not thought it derogatory to their dignity to exchange the sceptre for the trowel, have participated in our mysteries and joined in our assemblies. As a Freemason, I would first recommend to your most serious contemplation the Volume of the Sacred Law,

***Slide 8** (VSL)*

charging you to consider it the unerring standard of truth and justice and to regulate your actions by the Divine precepts it contains. As a citizen of the world, I enjoin you to be exemplary in the discharge of your civil duties: by never proposing or at all countenancing any act which may have a tendency to subvert the peace and good order of society. As an individual, I would further recommend the practice of every domestic as well as public virtue. Let prudence direct you, temperance chasten you, fortitude support you and justice be the guide of all your actions. Still, as a Freemason, there are other excellencies of character to which your attention may be directed. Among the foremost of these are secrecy, fidelity and obedience.

***Slide 9** (Aude, vide, tace)*

Secrecy consists in an inviolable adherence to the obligation you have entered upon, never improperly to disclose any of those Masonic secrets which have now been or may at any future time be entrusted to your keeping.

Your fidelity must be exemplified by a close conformity to the constitutions of the Fraternity and by refraining from recommending anyone to a participation in our secrets unless you have strong grounds to believe that he will reflect honour on our choice. Your obedience must be proved by modest and correct demeanour in the Lodge; by abstaining from every topic of religious or political discussion and by a ready acquiescence in all votes and resolutions duly passed by a majority of the brethren.

And as a last general recommendation, I exhort you to dedicate yourself to such pursuits as may enable you to continue respectable in life, useful to mankind and an ornament to that society of which you have this day become a member.

ST nods to Mr UV who is guided to return the nod by ADC who guides Mr UV to his seat. Deacons square the lodge and return to their seats.

Precep.   Thankyou brethren – and thank you Mr UV. *(All sit)*

Slide 10 *(Burns)*

Master   Many famous men have been Freemasons – government leaders, sportsmen, comedians, military men, explorers, musicians, and poets. One of the most famous poet Freemasons was the Immortal Bard, Robert Burns. You will remember many of his poems and songs – *My love is like a red, red rose; Green grow the rashes O; The silver Tassie; Ae fond kiss* and of course the *Address to a haggis.*

Bro. Robert Burns was initiated into Freemasonry in 1781. He remained a committed Freemason for the rest of his tragically short life. Here is a poem he wrote about Brotherly Love, entitled *John Anderson my Jo*. As a rare treat, it will be read to you in Burns' own tongue by our Brother XY who is a Scot. *(XY reads the poem from his place and then sits.)*

Master   Thankyou Bro. XY. Ladies and gentlemen, you will find a translation in your packs.

Slide 11 *(Kipling)*

Master   Rudyard Kipling was initiated in 1858 into a lodge in India, one supported by both British and Indian communities. Here is Kipling's most Masonic poem, *The Mother Lodge*, recalling the brotherly love he experienced in India. It is read by Bro. ZA *(Reads Kipling's poem or a selection of stanzas from it. The slides going with each stanza are pictures from 19th century India. The slides accompanying the chorus set out the words with an invitation to the audience to join it. It would be great to use the jumping red dot!* **Slides 12 to 27**.*)*

Secretary Thankyou Brother ZA *(Pause)* We started this sequence talking about famous Freemasons and we have prepared a little quiz for you.

Slide 28 *(Some famous Freemasons)*

You will find a copy in your pack, with some clues. The guest who gets the most answers correct will be awarded a bottle of bubbly. I now call upon Bro. BC to tell us something about the history of Freemasonry.

Slide 29 *(Picture of castle)*

BC There are several theories about the origins of Freemasonry. The difference between them turns largely on the connection, if any, between *operative* and *speculative* masons.

The word *operative* describes working masons who actually worked with stone. The trade of the working mason peaked with the building of the great castles and cathedrals from the 12th to the 15th century. To take an example, the construction in 1290 of Beaumaris Castle on Anglesey in North Wales, involved 400 masons, 2,000 labourers, 200 quarrymen and 30 smiths and carpenters together with 100 carts, 60 wagons and 30 boats. Masons working on such buildings created lodges, or shelters at the building site or quarry in which to talk, exchange views and no doubt complain about the Master Mason and their pay.

Slide 30 *(Working masons)*

In the middle ages masons went through an apprenticeship at the end of which they were considered qualified – or *free*. The word is still met in the title *Freeman of the City of London*. Since they worked hard to become qualified, quite understandably, they did not want unqualified workers – sometimes called *cowans* – taking their jobs. Since few people could read and write at that time, certificates were of little use and so masons used signs and passwords to prove that they were qualified, and they kept these secret for obvious reasons.

Slide 31 *(Pictures of early speculative Freemasons)*

At some point in time, men who were not working masons joined lodges. This seems to have happened first in Scotland

and it is the beginning of what we call *speculative* masonry. The old word *speculative* describes someone who ponders on, or speculates about, the meaning of things. The speculative Mason uses the tools and practices of masonry as symbols for moral teaching.

So this theory of the origins of Freemasonry is known as the *transitional* theory. It is a theory of a gradual transition from operative masonry to speculative Freemasonry.

Slide 32 *(English civil war)*

Other masonic thinkers disagree with this theory. They see speculative Freemasonry as being a brand new creation, arising in the 16th or 17th centuries in reaction to the religious troubles of the time. Just think of Henry VIII, Bloody Mary, the beheading of Charles I, Cromwell and the Jacobite rebellions. Well-meaning men of different creeds, may have sought secret ways to meet together.

Slide 33 *(Humorous picture of spy)*

In this theory, the secrets of Freemasonry, the words and signs, were not to protect jobs but to protect the members from spies. The talk of the mason's trade was mainly 'cover'. The fact that from its very beginning, speculative Freemasonry has been open to men of all religions may be evidence for this, and we still forbid all religious and political discussion in Lodge.

Slide 34 *(James I)*

During the 17th century, we see the spread of speculative Freemasonry. There is a view that King James VI of Scotland (later James I of England) was accepted into a Scottish Lodge in 1601.[61] From 1620, there is evidence of men who were not operatives joining the London Company of Masons. This was called the *Acception* and is where part of our name comes from: *Free and Accepted Masons*.

Slide 35 *(Elias Ashmole and the museum)*

In 1646, Elias Ashmole, whose name lives on in the Ashmolean Museum in Oxford, was made a Freemason in Warrington, Cheshire. In 1691, the celebrated diarist John Aubrey made a note that:

---

[61] Lodge Scoon and Perth No. 3 in Perth, but the record of this event dates from 1658.

> *This day ... is a great convention at St. Paul's Church of the fraternity of the Accepted masons where Sir Christopher Wren is to be adopted a brother: and Sir Henry Goodric of ye tower, & divers others ...*

Slide 36 *(Goose and Gridiron)*

In 1717, nearly 300 years ago, the modern organisation of Freemasonry begins with the first Grand Lodge. Four Lodges in London met at the *Goose and Gridiron* tavern in St Paul's Churchyard *and resolv'd to hold an annual assembly and feast.* Modern Freemasonry grew from there. (*BC exchanges nods with Chaplain and returns to his seat*).

Slide 37 *(Tell the story of your lodge.)*

Sec. I will ask Bro. DE to speak about the early days of ... Lodge. (*DE goes to the podium.*)

DE The Founders of our Lodge were *(jobs)*. Today, there is a similar mix of backgrounds in the lodge. We have *(jobs)*. Whatever we are, we are equal as brothers. External rank and fortune is not the least important to us.

Slide 38 *(Pictures of Freemasons around the world)*

A brother's colour, race or religion is not important either. Freemasonry is open to all and so is ... Lodge. Freemasonry has welcomed Christians, Jews, Hindus, Muslims, Deists, Catholics and Protestants. ... Lodge extends the same welcome. (*DE returns to his seat.*)

(*Eight slides **39-46** allocated to illustrate lodge history.*)

Sec I will now ask our Treasurer to talk about the financial side.

Treasurer goes to the podium and exchanges nods with Chaplain.

Slide 47 *(pie chart)*

This section will obviously be amended to be relevant to your lodge.

Treas. It costs about £££ a year to run the Lodge. The main costs are the lodge dinners, the Festive Boards (here in light yellow); the dues we pay to Grand Lodge (light blue); those we pay to Provincial Grand Lodge (maroon) and the rent of the temple (light green.) The Lodge maintains a reserve of about £££ to fund the operations of the Lodge, to cover any loss that we may make in a year — and, of course, to pay for my annual holiday in Monte Carlo!

Slide 48 *(Picture of caravan in the rain)*

> The reserve fund pays for repairs and purchases which used to include the breast jewel given to the Master at the end of his year, but it is now the custom for a Past Master to return his jewel when given Provincial Grand Rank.

Slide 49 *(PM jewel)*

> The jewel is refurbished and a new Past Master's name added to those of his predecessors already engraved on it. The jewels thus become objects of historical interest. *(Choose one of special interest.)* Bro. FG *(stands)* wears one of our most famous and most valuable jewels … *(FG describes then sits.)*

Slide 50 *(Money bag)*

> The cost of running the lodge in the year to come is estimated and this amount divided between the brethren. Each pays his share (called his *dues*) before the year starts. Sometimes we make a small excess and sometimes a loss, which is why we keep a reserve fund.

Slide 51 *(Trowel)*

> Charity is one of our ideals and each brother is expected to give. How much? Well as much as the brother's situation in life may fairly warrant. How much does the lodge itself give?

Slide 52 *(Charity logos)*

> Well, taking the year … as an example, the Lodge gave £££ to the Grand Charity, £££ to Little Havens Children's Hospice and £££ to Leukaemia Research. We put £££ into our Widows Fund and found £££ to support the local Music School concert. While some of this money came from Lodge reserves and Lodge events, x% came directly from the pockets of the brethren. *(Use your own charitable examples, of course. These are given only for guidance.)*

Slide 53 *(Charity logos)*

> We have also supported other non-Masonic causes — including the British Epilepsy Association, Macmillan Nurses, Havering Association for People with Disabilities, the British Heart Foundation and Essex Air Ambulance. I don't say this to boast. I tell you this to demonstrate how important charity is in our Masonic lives. *(Ditto)*

Slide 54 *(Golf picture)*

As I said, some of the charity money is raised through Lodge events ... *(Give relevant examples)*

Bro. Kevin, our Charity Steward (left), takes a moment at the annual golf day

Slide 55 *(photo from Charity Ball)*

    Our Ladies Festival raises £££ as well as being lots of fun. Of course, our Lodge plays its part in the charitable life of the Masonic Province. We are a Double Grand Patron etc. etc.

Slide 56 *(Charity logos)*

    At national level, Freemasonry is second only to the Lottery in charitable giving. The Grand Charity is the largest of the Masonic charities. It gives money to assist Masons in distress, and their widows and children but 50% of it goes to non-Masonic causes. The Grand Charity supports The Royal College of Surgeons, Mencap, Research into Ageing, Drug Abuse, Hospices and many other charities large and small. We are fortunate that through our fraternal Grand Lodges overseas, we can provide emergency aid very quickly to places in the world hit by disaster.

Treasurer exchanges nods with Chaplain and returns to his seat.

Slide 57 *(Almoner collar jewel)*

Sec   I will ask our Almoner, to talk about support for our own folk.

Almoner goes to the podium and exchanges nods with Chaplain.

Alm My job is to be the eyes and ears of the Lodge. I seek to maintain contact with all Lodge widows, Lodge members and their dependants and to identify where help is required. Hence my collar jewel is a purse. *(Again what follows will be modified to fit your lodge.)*

We maintain a small Benevolent Fund for emergencies. We also maintain a fund for our widows. However, if a Brother or a Lodge widow needs major help — an operation, a stair lift, or financial support — the Almoner takes the matter up with one of the Masonic Charities. Such help is not always easy to get and is usually means tested but it is worth trying for.

Slide 58 (Masonic charities)

The main aim of the Grand Charity is to support Freemasons and their dependants who are experiencing hardship. This includes past, present and lapsed members of Lodges. It also includes widows and certain other immediate dependants of a Freemason. As a general guide, almost anyone related to a Freemason who receives Pension Credits or other means-tested benefits is likely to be eligible. Grand Charity also manages a scheme offering the free loan of mobility equipment such as stair lifts, scooters and wheelchairs.

The Royal Masonic Trust for Girls and Boys provides that education for the children of a Freemason as their fathers would have done, had they been able to do so. The Trust helps children who are at school, at college or university, or studying at postgraduate level.

The Masonic Samaritan Fund provides financial assistance to those who have to wait an unacceptably long time for NHS treatment but cannot afford private treatment.

The Royal Masonic Benevolent Institution operates residential care homes in England and Wales. Many homes are registered for both residential and nursing care and a number of them offer specialist dementia care. While charges are made for care and accommodation, unlike other such homes, once the assets of a resident fall below the critical amount, the Royal Masonic Benevolent Institution steps in and pays everything thereafter.

There are no age limits for such assistance and there is no requirement to still be active within the Craft. Indeed, we can often help even when a Freemason's membership has lapsed. Applications are welcome on behalf of the wife, partner, widow or surviving partner of a Freemason. Nearly 50% of the grants made by the Masonic Samaritan Fund have been in support of the wives, widows and dependants of Freemasons.

Slide 59 *(Almoner collar jewel)*

So Ladies, Gentlemen and Brethren, if you know of anyone who needs help do please let me know as soon as you can. At the very least speak to me and take one of my cards. You never know when help might be needed.

Almoner exchanges nods with Chaplain and returns to his seat.

Slide 60 *(Amusing picture about the battle of the sexes)*

Secretary Finally, since there are many ladies present, I will call upon our ADC to tell you about women and Freemasonry.

ADC goes to the podium and exchanges nods with Chaplain.

Ladies and gentlemen, Freemasonry is often thought to be a men only affair but ladies have always been involved. There never was a guild of masons as such, but a few of the larger cities did have guild-like bodies which tended to be religious fraternities with a social side.

Slide 61 *(Picture of 14th century fashion)*

One such was founded in 1313 in Lincoln and it seems that brothers and sisters were admitted. There were male and female members. The London Company of Freemasons held a regular Mass and afterwards a dinner (at what we would call lunch time) to which wives were invited. The price in 1481 was 12 old pence (about 5 new pence) which would have been 3 day's wages at the time.

Slide 62 *(Picture of 17th century fashion)*

The sons or daughters of a liveryman could claim membership. In 1663, a Margaret Wild was a member and as late as 1713 one Mary Banister of Barking was entered into articles. Today, the United Grand Lodge of England is a men only body and recognises as regular only those Grand Lodges which adopt certain principles, one of which reads:

A Bro. *stands and reads*

That membership of the Grand Lodge and individual Lodges shall be composed exclusively of men; and that each Grand Lodge shall have no Masonic intercourse of any kind with mixed Lodges or bodies which admit women to membership.

Bro. sits. ADC continues

If legends are to be believed, this has not stopped the initiation of women. Viscount Doneraile, a resident of Cork in the early part of the eighteenth century, held an occasional lodge in his own house.

Slide 63 *(Honourable Elizabeth St Leger)*

The story goes that one evening, his daughter, the Honourable Elizabeth St Leger, hid in the next room where some building work was going on. She is said to have removed a brick to witness the ceremony of initiation. However she aroused the suspicions of the Tyler who barred her get away with drawn sword and her scream brought members of the lodge rushing to the spot. After a considerable discussion she was initiated to safeguard the secrets and, to complete the story, later became the Master of the lodge. Fairy story or not, there is a plaque to the event in the Protestant Cathedral in Cork.

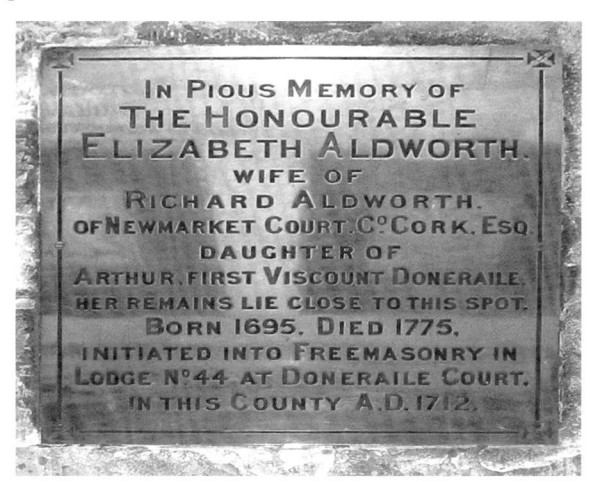

IN PIOUS MEMORY OF
THE HONOURABLE
ELIZABETH ALDWORTH.
WIFE OF
RICHARD ALDWORTH.
OF NEWMARKET COURT. CO CORK. ESQ
DAUGHTER OF
ARTHUR, FIRST VISCOUNT DONERAILE.
HER REMAINS LIE CLOSE TO THIS SPOT.
BORN 1695. DIED 1775.
INITIATED INTO FREEMASONRY IN
LODGE N° 44 AT DONERAILE COURT.
IN THIS COUNTY A.D. 1712.

Evidence has recently come to light of a female Masonic Lodge in Essex in 1787 and of a procession of lady Masons *dressed in white and purple* just over the river at Dartford, Kent in 1796. It is said that the Provincial Grand Master of Essex at the time actively promoted female Masonry. The only way was Essex, perhaps!

Slide 64 *(A picture of a lady Grand Master)*

        Women's Freemasonry is very active in many parts of the world and there are two orders in the UK, the Order of Women's Freemasonry, established in 1908 and the Honourable Fraternity of Ancient Freemasons established in 1913. We have with us this afternoon, two Grand Officers in the Order of Women's Freemasonry *(they stand)*: Mrs HI and JK. *(Ladies sit.) (Naturally, this depends upon the presence of such ladies.)*

Slide 65 *(A picture of centenary of Lady Freemasons)*

        Since 1998, the United Grand Lodge of England has recognised that the two English women's jurisdictions are regular in practice and has indicated that these bodies may be regarded as part of Freemasonry, when describing Freemasonry in general. The rituals of the women's orders are identical to ours.

ADC exchanges nods with Chaplain and returns to his seat.

Slide 66 *(A photo of a tray of champagne)*

Sec   Ladies, Gentlemen and Brethren. The WM will shortly bring this part of the proceedings to a close but before he does so, may I announce that free drinks will be waiting for you outside so there is no need to rush to the bar.

Slide 67 *(Lodge emblem again)*

WM   You are now about to quit this safe retreat of peace and friendship and mix again with the busy world. Amidst all its cares and employments, forget not those sacred duties which have been so frequently inculcated and so strongly recommended in this Lodge.

        Be ye therefore discreet, prudent, and temperate. Remember that at this pedestal you have solemnly and voluntarily vowed to relieve and befriend with unhesitating cordiality every Brother who might need your assistance; that you have promised to remind him in the most gentle manner of his failings and to aid and vindicate his character whenever wrongfully traduced; to suggest the most candid, the most palliating and the most favourable circumstances, even when his conduct is justly liable to reprehension and blame. Thus shall the world see how dearly Freemasons love each other.

But, my brethren, you are expected to extend these noble and generous sentiments still further. Let me impress upon your minds, and may it be instilled into your hearts, that every human creature has a just claim on your kind offices. I therefore trust that you will be good to all. More particularly do I recommend to your care the household of the faithful, that by diligence and fidelity in the duties of your respective vocations, liberal beneficence and diffusive charity, by constancy and sincerity in your friendships; a uniformly kind, just, amiable and virtuous deportment, prove to the world the happy and beneficial effects of our ancient and honourable institution.

Let it not be said that you laboured in vain nor wasted your strength for nought; for your work is before the Lord and your recompense is with God. Finally brethren, be of one mind, live in peace and may the God of love and mercy delight to dwell amongst you and bless you for evermore.

Brother in chair gavels. Music starts. Deacons move to position.

ADC   Ladies and Gentlemen, please stand while the WM, accompanied by his lady, his Wardens and their ladies, the Past Deputy Provincial Grand Master of Flanders, Grand Officers and their escorts, leave the Lodge. Forward, brethren. *(Usual exit.)*

Openness and the White Table

> *Now I shout it from the highest hills*
> *Even told the golden daffodils*
> *At last my heart's an open door*
> *And my secret love's no secret anymore*
>
> Tina Ann Barrett, Tim Laws, Thomas Mark Harmer Nicholls. Sung by Doris Day

Some brethren may be anxious about the propriety of a White Table but the secrecy which quite unnecessarily surrounds our order today is a fairly recent innovation. While public appearances of Masons do occur in the UK, they are far less common than in earlier times. During the 18th century, it was common for a lodge to process to and from church on St John's Day, the typical day for installation of the WM.

Processions are far more common in North America. Here are the rules observed by Texas Masons in the 1920s:

> *The following General Rules to be observed in Masonic processions ... Too much attention cannot be paid to public processions. They should always appear in strict order, and the course of the procession should be in straight lines, and all turns at right angles. Brethren walking two and two may either be with locked arms or with elbows touching, and the divisions of two should be at six feet distance from each other. When music is used, attention should be paid to keeping the step. It is proper that brethren who appear as Master Masons should wear white gloves and white sashes in all processions, though blue sashes may be used. Brethren should always be clothed according to the degree they assume in the procession ... Brethren in procession ought always to be dressed in black coat, hat and pantaloons.*[62]

In small towns in the USA and Canada, the annual parade would not be complete without an appearance of the Shriners,[63] the fun end of Masonry in North America. With their tiny cars and motor bikes, accompanying their *Potentate* often riding in a 1960s Cadillac convertible, they raise huge sums of money to support their hospitals for children in Canada, the USA and Panama.

---

[62] From the Official Monitor of the Grand Lodge of Ancient Free and Accepted Masons of the State of Texas, 1922.

[63] *Ancient Arabic Order of the Nobles of the Mystic Shrine*, open to all Freemasons in North America.

You may have come across black rosettes in an old regalia case. At one time fixed over the rosettes or levels on the apron to denote mourning, their use is now very uncommon in England where there are no Masonic funerals. In 1962, the United Grand Lodge said that there may:

... be no active participation by Masons, as such, in any part of the burial service or cremation of a Brother and that there be no Masonic prayers, readings or exhortations either then or at the graveside subsequent to the internment, since the final obsequies of any human being, Mason or not, are complete in themselves and do not call in the case of a Freemason for any additional

137

> *ministrations. That if it is wished to recall and allude to his Masonic life and actions, this can appropriately be done at the next lodge meeting in the presence of his brethren, or at a specifically arranged Memorial Service.*

Despite this, mention of the deceased's Masonic life is still commonly made and my own father's coffin carried a square and compasses. In North America, Masonic funerals are frequently carried out. The Statutes of the Grand Lodge of Montana state:

> *Every Master Mason and every Entered Apprentice and Fellow Craft Mason who has been prevented by death from further advancement, who dies while in good standing is entitled to burial with Masonic honors.*

Oddly enough, a number of Grand Lodges in the USA forbid Masonic obsequies to Fellow Crafts and Entered Apprentices, although the Grand Lodge of Massachusetts, says:

> *No Mason shall be interred with the formalities of the Order, unless it be at his own special request, made known to the Lodge during his lifetime or communicated to its officers after his death by a family member, an intimate friend, or other credible person, nor unless he has been advanced to the degree of Master Mason and was in good standing at the time of his death, without a Dispensation from the Grand Master.*

But then goes on:

> *We have been instructed that if the family requests a Masonic funeral service, we are to provide it, NO QUESTION, and the matter of his standing will be "healed" later by the Grand Master. We are not to quibble at a time of grieving of the family.*

Clearly, in North America, Masonry is very much a public matter but here in the UK, we are at last beginning to reverse the secretiveness which has dogged us since perhaps the 1920s. London Freemasons now march in the Lord Mayor's parade and the annual procession to church still occurs in Warwickshire:

> *The present Vicar of St Mary's, The Revd Dr Vaughan Roberts, welcomed everyone to the service during which representatives of the Jewish, Sikh, Islamic, Hindu and Christian faiths offered thoughts and blessings relating to the theme of the multi-denominational service, "Brotherly Love and Charity".*

> *Conducted by the Provincial Grand Chaplain W Bro John Cowan (sic!), together with the Assistant Grand Chaplain W Bro Paul Wheeler, the service included Lessons read by VW Bro Alan Wellan, Deputy Provincial Grand Master, and the RW Bro David Macey, Provincial Grand Master, with the Provincial Choir, conducted by W Bro Roy Marshall, demonstrating its professionalism by singing moving anthems.*[64]

While opinions differ, our fraternity is not a secret and there is no reason why we should be secretive about it. After all, Freemasons' Hall in Great Queen Street is not only highly visible, it is used as a film set and a venue for fashion catwalks. Of course, we do have secrets, and they are important. Our motto is after all *Aude, Vide, Tace* — hear, see and be silent.[65] While our secrets are nothing more sinister than formal words and signs of recognition, they are not revealed to non-masons, even though most of them are known to dogs taken for walks. Why do we retain them? There are many reasons.

There is that old reason, tradition. The masonic secrets go back many centuries. They may once have had a practical use — proof of holding a qualification in the masons' trade or passwords to fool spies, depending which theory of the derivation of Freemasonry you hold to — and having held these secrets for some 360 years and being committed to continuity with the past and future as we are, we hold them dear. The ability to keep a secret is also a virtue and masonry is about the inculcation of morality.

However, the most powerful reason is that the secrets control access to the various steps in Freemasonry, making each just that little bit more exciting. Knowing the secrets before completing the next step would be a bit like opening your presents before your birthday. What you get is the same but it does not feel the same and it must be acknowledged that the mystery of the secrets is a part of the attraction, part of the thrill in joining. Owning the secrets produces a feeling of belonging, satisfying what psychologists call a need for affiliation. Mystery may attract or repel but the secrets we have remain central to Freemasonry.

Nevertheless, what is secret is not our fraternity, not our aprons or collars, not even our ritual, which can be bought quite freely over the

---

[64] *Freemasonry Today*, December 2012.

[65] Advice which might well be more generally heeded when instant revelations on social networks get so many people into trouble.

counter or online,[66] but the tokens and words of the degrees. What is definitely not secret is the brotherly love, relief and truth which we should talk about and demonstrate whenever we can. All of which means that White Tables are perfectly respectable.

By the way, while it is necessary to get a dispensation to appear in public in Masonic clothing, this never seems to apply to a White Table.

ಐ ಐ ಐ

Happy guests make a happy meeting.

---

[66] Even from Letchworths, the shop in Freemasons' Hall. Oddly enough, Letchworths refused to stock my earlier book, *The Goat, the Devil and the Freemason* because they thought that the cover would give non-Masons the wrong idea!

Success

> *Here comes success, here comes success.*
> *Over my hill, over my hill.*
> *Here comes success, here comes success.*
> *Well, here comes my car, here comes my car,*
> *Here comes my Chinese rug, here comes my Chinese rug,*
> *Here comes success, here comes success.*
>
> <small>Shawn Carter, Nasir Jones, Ernest Wilson, Larry Ellis. Sung by Iggy Pop.</small>

A lodge that feels good about itself is a lodge that can welcome and try out new ideas. A lodge that is known for new ideas is an exciting lodge and one that gets talked about.

> We were recently asked to help a lodge that was in a bad way. It hadn't had any work to do for some time and the members were becoming despondent. We created, rehearsed and delivered a ninety minute show about the history of the lodge, with songs, music, film and a cast of around twenty five, drawn from the lodge and its antecedents. The temple was packed and the lodge dined around 100 brethren and guests. The lodge became the talk of the town. (One member of the cast was made an Assistant Provincial Grand Master, though to be honest it might not have been only because he appeared in the show!) Shortly after that we offered the lodge some of our work. They turned us down because they had their own candidates.

The web

A warning: a website is part of the process, not the complete solution. Unless your lodge is doing interesting things, it will have nothing to talk about. With nothing to talk about, your website will be static and boring — and no one will respond to it.

The old saying that if you invent a better mousetrap, the world will beat a path to you door, is of course completely false. If you are doing something worthwhile, you have to go out and tell the world about it.

In many people's eyes, the web is a new and evolving phenomenon. To other people, it is old hat! Whatever it is, the web is generally the first port of call for information today — and so it makes sense for us to use it to tell people about ourselves.

There is bound to be someone in your lodge who can create and maintain a website. Our website was expertly created by Lawrie Morrisson who also puts in many happy hours maintaining it (with my interference.) You may not have his skills but you can still produce something worth looking at and the benefits can be great:

- A website is free or almost so. You can host a site for around £30 a year or even less.

- Many hosting sites offer tools to help you create your website with the minimum of know-how. These hosting sites cost a bit more but are worth it. With some skill in word processing and page lay-out, you can create a website in a day or two.

- Unlike magazines which soon disappear from sight (or into dentists' waiting rooms), a website is there all the time, for as long as you pay your hosting subscription.

- If you have something interesting to offer, the web crawlers will find and list you — and people will come to you as a result.

- In general, younger people are more likely to use the web. This is all to the good. Freemasonry is ageing and we need younger men to join us and younger men know other younger men — and know how to talk to them.

- Your website is much more than an advert. It will put our message out; combat the silly accusations that are made about us and state what we stand for. The more of us who do that, the louder and clearer the message becomes.

Your website becomes an open door for people wanting to join and there really are many people out there who want to join us;

- people who share our values
- who believe in brotherly love, relief and truth
- who want what we offer
- and who are willing to make a commitment.

In the month of January 2014 alone, the St Laurence Lodge website received 12,000 hits, almost half of what the website of the United Grand Lodge of England itself received. The effect has been that in the last three years the web has brought us 47 enquiries regarding membership. We also received three from the more usual route of existing members. Of these, eleven have already become members (two joining members and nine initiates) and several are still in play, so to speak, and new contacts occur all the time. Even more importantly, we are starting to get second generation candidates, friends of those who initially joined us via the web. We currently have a waiting list of ten and this is just *one* website of *one* lodge in *one* small corner of England.

The eleven who joined us have been wonderful additions to our lodge. Because they sought us out, because they had researched our order, they already knew a great deal about Freemasonry and they knew it was for them. Once they joined, they set about developing their Masonic knowledge without delay.

A very special initiation: a 'man of the cloth' is initiated by an invited team including the Provincial Grand Chaplain.

Not that easy

The 47 contacts via the web were from people who were complete strangers. Why did they came to us? Idly curious, testing us out, wanting to know more, seeking what we offer, wanting to join? For all those reasons but no matter what reason, there was something about our website which attracted them.

Do remember that a website is only a blank page. You need interesting stories to fill it and a flow of interesting stories to keep keep readers coming back. As a guideline, add something new at least once a week — especially pictures.

Designing the website

What should a website look like? Do take some time to study our site at www.stlaurencelodge.org.uk. Here are some pointers:

The right hand moving column — websites have be kept up to date. If not, possible candidates will lose interest in you and so will the search engines. People who may become candidates are unlikely to respond to your website on first viewing. They may come back several times before taking the plunge. If the site is constantly being updated, such folk will see your lodge as active and interesting.

The central column — where we highlight the latest and most interesting events. People like to click on something that catches their eye almost as soon as landing on the site.

Join Us — links to a page to answer possible questions and invite more. Note how this is done by links and not by a mass of typeface.

Events — lots of pictures and not too many words. Obviously you need the permission of brethren in the photos before publishing but blanket permission prevents having to ask each time. A few brethren did decline and a few did not want their surnames used but most had no objections.

Contacts — always to the Secretary, no name. One has to be careful.

No clay pigeon is safe from these brethren!

We also have a *quiz*, a bit of *history*, some information on some of our *publications* and some *news* items, among other material.

On the website, we report what is going on, aiming as I have said, for an update at least once a week and usually more frequently. We report our own meetings, interesting visits to other lodges, our social and sporting events[67] and, where possible, the activities of individual members. To repeat, you need more than a website to attract candidates. You need a website that belongs to an interesting lodge, doing interesting things.

Anyway, you will design your own site. I do hope so. The more frequently good people are invited to join Freemasonry, the less we will be seen as an elite apart. If anyone can join, and within limits anyone can, then Freemasons must be normal folk, just like us.

Managing contacts

To get to know the people who contact us, we arrange informal events — a visit to Freemasons Hall, a tour of the British Museum, a drink at a convenient pub or a dinner at a Chinese restaurant. We do this about ten times a year and each candidate will have attended at least four such events and had other conversations with brethren before we offer him a Form P. Our rule for contacts from the website is that a year must elapse between first contact and initiation. (Candidates who come via the more traditional route, being friends or relations of brethren, will wait less time, as they are already known by a brother.)

Contacts do have to be managed carefully. It is a mistake to think that everyone who looks at a website, takes in everything that is said. A simple example is geography. We learned early on that the names of towns and counties are repeated all over the world. We invited one contact to join us at an event in Upminster, Essex. A couple of days beforehand, he wrote saying while he knew Essex well, he did not know Upminster. Alarm bells rang and we worked out that he lived in the Essex just outside Baltimore in the USA. Although the website says that we are in the UK, people can miss this.

I have been using the word 'people' instead of 'men' for a reason. Our website says that we are an all male lodge but nevertheless we have had contacts from ladies. We are fortunate that we know a couple of Grand Officers in the Women's Order of Freemasonry, so that we are able to pass such contacts on to them.

---

[67] *Events*: charity golf day, golf match, garden party, ladies' festival, quiz night, St George's Day supper, Freemasons' Hall with lunch, British Museum with lunch, round table at a Chinese restaurant, pizza supper, dinner at East End Indian restaurant, White Table, summer party, charity ball, ten pin bowling.

Caution

So far we have had no major problems but it does pay to be careful. No addresses appear on our website or in our emails. We always make initial contact in public places and our communication is by email — not telephone — until we are sure to whom we are talking.

Occasionally, we will find that a contact is not appropriate and we have to say this clearly but politely. Sometimes, the contact is looking for more than we can offer, perhaps even psychological help. We are fortunate that we can readily obtain professional advice on how to respond in such cases but good manners, human understanding, openness and the five points of fellowship go a long way.

Some make contact and then fade away. Sometimes we get no response to our initial email. One never knows why but it could always mean that the original contact was from a person who did not wish us well. So our initial reply has to be carefully written but, needless to say, always remains polite and friendly. Its actual contents will of course depend upon what the original contact writes, but here is a generic example:

> Many thanks for your enquiry about Freemasonry and our Lodge. It is always a pleasure to hear from men who share our values and always enjoyable to meet those who might decide to join us.
>
> Our happy lodge is open to all men, no matter their creed, status, colour or sexual preference. We have black and white members — some well to do, others less so — and our ages vary from under thirty to over eighty. (We would not normally initiate anyone under the age of twenty-one.)
>
> If you've browsed our website you'll know that to be a Freemason, a man must be of good character and believe in a Supreme Being, although your religious beliefs are your concern alone. You will have seen that there are time commitments and costs, including charitable donations, joining and membership fees. It would be useful if you would confirm that you can comply with all this.
>
> We hold four regular meetings a year in Upminster and our lodge of instruction (which runs weekly from September to May) is in Hornchurch, so it would be best if you are within fairly easy reach of these towns. If you live at a distance from us, you may prefer to join a lodge nearer to your home or place of work. We can put you in touch with one, should you so wish.

We occasionally receive enquiries from people abroad who do not realise we are based in England so it is worth repeating this now. We are an all male lodge, as are all lodges under the United Grand Lodge of England. If, as a woman, you wish to become a Freemason, we would be delighted to put you in touch with the wonderful Order of Women Freemasons.

You will eventually need a proposer and a seconder but the first step is meet our members, quite informally. We can discuss your interest and, if all goes well, we will invite you to some of our social events so that we get to know each other better. We invest the time because you and the lodge must be sure that the decision for you to join is the right one. It is not a decision to be taken lightly; not like joining a club — more like making a life choice.

Once you and the lodge have decided to proceed, two members who have come to know you will be delighted to propose and second you to be initiated into Freemasonry and become a member of our lodge. The whole process will take about a year. If you would prefer a chat to start with, email me your telephone number and let me know the best time to call you.

I should tell you that there are other lodges who are short of new members and where progress might be speedier. We are fortunate enough to be a very successful lodge and have a waiting list but we can introduce you to other lodges if you so wish.

In any case, perhaps you would confirm you are able to comply with the requirements mentioned in this email and tell us something about yourself. Thanks for writing to us and we look forward to hearing from you and meeting you soon.

Mentoring

In some lodges and chapters, the role of Mentor is not treated as seriously as it might be, but in our strategy, mentoring is vital. Remember that many of our new initiates were strangers when they first contacted us and so we start the mentoring process as soon as a contact comes to meet us. From then on, we ensure that all contacts, candidates and new initiates are monitored.

We make sure that all new contacts are introduced to members, other contacts and candidates. At our informal dinners, we play 'general post'; moving senior brethren around the table so that each gets to meet every new contact and candidate. We keep an eagle eye on everyone new to us to ensure that they are involved in the conversation. At some point, a senior brother will start asking them about Masonry — what they know and what they would like to know — and will answer all their questions frankly and openly.

New brethren

We are careful with our Festive Board table plans, making sure that no one gets left out on a limb, seating newer members next to different brethren at each meeting, so extending their knowledge of the membership at large. We make sure that at Lodge of Instruction (LOI), new members are given a job to do right from the start. Once they are Master Masons, we get them in the chair to get a feel for things.

At the LOI, we try to avoid just running through the ritual. Of course, the Master will want to practise his bits as the meeting nears but at other occasions, we focus on the deacons' work, on opening and closing, on the Inner Guard's role etc., repeating passages until newer brethren are clear. We might run through the perambulations three or four times in an evening. We stop and explain the meaning of what is being rehearsed.

We hold occasional mentor's evenings when newer brethren are invited to come long and discuss matters which they might otherwise find difficult to raise, perhaps because they think the question might seem a silly one. We seek to emphasise that there are no silly questions; only things brethren want to know. Some questions are practical matters such as inviting guests to meetings or giving toasts at the festive board; some are about the history of our order; others are about meaning — of the ritual, the tools and the furnishings of the lodge.

We take new brethren out to visit other lodges, especially those with a ritual different from ours. The mentor always carries an EA and an FC apron together with a spare black tie and pair of gloves, just in case. It is no use working hard to get candidates, if you do not also work hard to keep them.

ಐ ಐ ಐ

A lodge may be led by a small group of brethren but it can never be successful unless the brethren at large are supportive and involved.

Triple!

Triple Initiation, 9 November 2013

Such was our waiting list that we thought it worthwhile to risk a triple initiation. While a normal initiation takes about an hour, we targeted our triple initiation at 90 minutes. We did not want to reduce the personal importance of the initiation for each candidate but we did want to minimise repetition. So, while we maintained the words of the ritual, we adapted the rubric.

It was the first time a triple initiation had been carried out by St Laurence Lodge in the whole of its 78 year history. A special dispensation was necessary from the Right Worshipful Provincial Grand Master of Essex to enable the ceremony to proceed and a cast of thousands (well quite a few) participated in the event.

Three Deacons were used, the third being denoted as D3, but the JD carried out all perambulations before the Obligation. We involved as many brethren as possible, with some Grand Officers for extra *gravitas*.

Section ONE — Entry and perambulations

T. *knocks of the C, having prepared Mr First*

IG *salute*.	Bro. JW. There is a report.
JW *salute*.	WM. There is a report.
WM	Bro. JW. Enquire who wants admission.
JW *cut S sit*.	Bro. IG. See who seeks admission.

IG *cut S. Goes to the door and opens it to ask questions of the T.*

IG	Whom have you there?
T	Mr *Given Names First*, a poor C in a state of d who has been well and worthily recommended, regularly proposed and approved in open lodge, now comes of his own free will and accord, properly prepared and humbly soliciting to be admitted to the m and p of Ancient Freemasonry.
IG	How does he hope to obtain those privileges?
T	By the help of God, being free and of good report.

IG *checks that the C is properly prepared. If he is, he proceeds:*

IG	Wait, while I report to the WM.
IG *locks door, goes p'ment, salute.*	WM. Mr *Given Names First*, a poor candidate in a state of d who has been well and worthily recommended, regularly proposed and approved in open Lodge, now comes of his own free will and accord, properly prepared and humbly soliciting to be admitted to the m and p of Ancient Freemasonry.
WM	How does he hope to obtain those privileges?
IG	By the help of God, being free and of good report.
WM	The tongue of good report has already been heard in his favour. Do you, Bro. IG, vouch that he is properly prepared?
IG	I do, WM.
WM	Admit him in due form. *(gavel)* Brother Ds.

IG cuts S, opens door when Ds are ready. Ds place kneeling stool on edge of p'ment. Go to door and take C, JD on C's right. IG applies p.

IG *to C*	Do you feel anything?
C *prompt JD*	Yes.

Ds guide C to kneeling stool. IG raises p above C's head.

WM *to C*	Mr *First* as no person can be made a Freemason unless he is free and of mature age, I demand, are you free and of the full age of twenty one years?
C *prompt JD*	I am.
WM	Then you will kneel while the blessing of heaven is invoked in aid of our proceedings.

Ds assist C to kneel, place his r h on his l b, t d. Raise wands in arch over C. S of R. WM gavels when C is kneeling. Brethren S of R.

Chaplain	Vouchsafe Thine aid, Almighty Father, Supreme Governor of the Universe, to our present convention and grant that this candidate for Freemasonry may so dedicate and devote his life to Thy service as to become a true and faithful Brother amongst us. Endue him with a competency of Thy divine wisdom so that, assisted by the secrets of our Masonic art, he may be the better enabled to unfold the beauties of true Godliness, to the honour and glory of Thy holy name.

Brethren	So mote it be.
WM	Mr *First*, in all cases of difficulty and danger, in whom do you put your trust?
C *prompt JD*	In God.
WM	Right glad am I to find your faith so well founded; relying on such sure support, you may safely rise and follow your leader with a firm but humble confidence, for where the name of God *(Brethren drop S)* is invoked, we trust no danger will ensue. *(WM and then brethren sit. C stands. SD removes kneeling stool.)*
WM *gavel*	Brethren in the N, E, S and W, take notice that Mr *Given Names First* is about to pass in view before you to show that he is a Candidate properly prepared to be made a Freemason.
JD	Step off with the left foot.

Grips C with his l hand behind the C's right forearm, guides C past WM to JW pedestal. With the C's r h, strikes the JW three times on the r s. SD follows to his seat.

JW *to JD.*	Whom have you there?
JD *salute*	Mr *Given Names First,* a poor candidate in a state of d who has been well and worthily recommended, regularly proposed and approved in open Lodge, now comes of his own free will and accord, properly prepared and humbly soliciting to be admitted to the m and p of Ancient Freemasonry.
JW	How does he hope to obtain those privileges?
JD	By the help of God, *(cut S)* being free and of good report.
JW stands	*(grasps C's r h in both his)* Enter, free and of good report. *(Sits.)*

JD waits until JW sits. Moves C back to pavement, then to right of SW. With the C's r h, strikes the SW three times on the r s.

SW *To JD.*	Whom have you there?
JD *salute*	Mr *Given Names First*, a poor Candidate in a state of d who has been well and worthily recommended, regularly proposed and approved in open Lodge, now

152

JD *(cont.)*	comes of his own free will and accord, properly prepared and humbly soliciting to be admitted to the m and p of Ancient Freemasonry.
SW	How does he hope to obtain those privileges?
JD	By the help of God, *(cuts S)* being free and of good report.
SW *stands*	(*grasps C's r h in both his*) Enter, free and of good report. (*Remains standing*.)

JD guides C to the NW corner. Turns C so that SW can take C's r h. Squares C to face WM. Lets go of C and steps back.

SW *raise C's r h, salute*.	WM. I present to you Mr *Given Names First*, a Candidate properly prepared to be made a Freemason.
WM	Bro. SW. *(salute)* Your presentation shall be attended to in due time. Meanwhile, you will instruct our Bro. JD to escort Mr *First* from the lodge for a while.
SW	Bro. JD, (*salute*) it is the Master's command that you escort Mr *First* from the lodge for a while. *(JD escorts First out.)*

T. Knocks of the Can, having prepared Mr Second.

IG *salute*	Bro. JW. There is a report. *(Holds S.)*
JW *salute*	WM. There is a report.
WM	Bro. JW. Enquire who wants admission.
JW *cuts S, sit*	Bro. IG. See who seeks admission.

IG cuts S. Goes to the door and opens it to ask questions of the T.

IG	Whom have you there?
T	Mr *Given Names Second*, a poor candidate in a state of d who has been well and worthily recommended, regularly proposed and approved in open Lodge, now comes of his own free will and accord, properly prepared and humbly soliciting to be admitted to the mysteries and privileges of Ancient Freemasonry.
IG	How does he hope to obtain those privileges?
T	By the help of God, being free and of good report.

IG checks that the C is properly prepared. If he is, he proceeds:

IG	Wait, while I report to the WM.

153

IG *locks door, goes p'ment, salute.*	WM. Mr *Given Names Second*, a poor candidate in a state of d who has been well and worthily recommended, regularly proposed and approved in open Lodge, now comes of his own free will and accord, properly prepared and humbly soliciting to be admitted to the m and p of Ancient Freemasonry.
Guest GO 1 *from beside WM pedestal*	How does he hope to obtain those privileges?
IG	By the help of God, being free and of good report.
Guest GO 1	The tongue of good report has already been heard in his favour. Do you, Bro. IG, vouch that he is properly prepared?
IG	I do.
Guest GO 1	Admit him in due form. *(WM gavel)* Brother Ds.

IG cuts S, opens door when Ds are ready. Ds place kneeling stool on edge of p'ment. Go to door and take C, JD on C's right. IG applies p.

IG *to C*	Do you feel anything?
C *prompt JD*	Yes.

Ds guide C to kneeling stool. IG raises p above C's head.

Guest GO 1 *to C*	Mr *Second*, as no person can be made a Freemason unless he is free and of mature age, I demand, are you free and of the full age of twenty one years?
C *prompt JD*	I am.
Guest GO 1	Then you will kneel while the blessing of heaven is invoked in aid of our proceedings.

Ds assist the C to kneel, his r h on his l b, t d. Raise wands in arch over C. S of R. WM Gavels when C is kneeling. Brethren S of R.

Chaplain	Vouchsafe Thine aid, Almighty Father, Supreme Governor of the Universe, to our present convention and grant that this candidate for Freemasonry may so dedicate and devote his life to Thy service as to become a true and faithful Brother amongst us.

Chaplain *(cont.)*	Endue him with a competency of Thy divine wisdom so that, assisted by the secrets of our Masonic art, he may be the better enabled to unfold the beauties of true Godliness, to the honour and glory of Thy holy name.
Brethren	So mote it be.
Guest GO 1	Mr *Second*, in all cases of difficulty and danger, in whom do you put your trust?
C *Prompt JD*	In God.
Guest GO 1	Right glad am I to find your faith so well founded; relying on such sure support, you may safely rise and follow your leader with a firm but humble confidence, for where the name of God *(All drop S)* is invoked, we trust no danger will ensue. *(C stands. SD removes kneeling stool. Brethren sit.)*
WM *gavel*	
Guest GO 1	Brethren in the N, E, S and W, take notice that Mr *Given Names Second* is about to pass in view before you to show that he is a candidate properly prepared to be made a Freemason. *(GO 1 sits.)*
JD	Step off with the left foot.

Grips C with his l hand behind the C's right forearm, guides C past WM, to JW pedestal. With the C's r h, strikes the JW three times on the r s. SD follows to his seat.

JW *to JD*.	Whom have you there?
JD s*alute*	Mr *Given Names Second*, a poor candidate in a state of d who has been well and worthily recommended, regularly proposed and approved in open Lodge, now comes of his own free will and accord, properly prepared and humbly soliciting to be admitted to the m and p of Ancient Freemasonry.
JW	How does he hope to obtain those privileges?
JD	By the help of God, *(cuts S)* being free and of good report.
JW s*tands*	*(grasps C's r h in both his)* Enter, free and of good report. (Sits.)

JD waits until JW sits. Moves C back to pavement, then to right of SW. With the C's r h, strikes the SW three times on the r s.

SW *to JD.*	Whom have you there?
JD *salutes*	Mr *Given Names Second*, a poor candidate in a state of d who has been well and worthily recommended, regularly proposed and approved in open Lodge, now comes of his own free will and accord, properly prepared and humbly soliciting to be admitted to the mysteries and privileges of Ancient Freemasonry.
SW	How does he hope to obtain those privileges?
JD	By the help of God, *(cuts S)* being free and of good report.
SW *stands*	*(grasps C's r h in both his)* Enter, free and of good report. *(Remains standing.)*

JD guides C to the NW corner. Turns C so that SW can take C's r h. Squares C to face WM. Lets go of C and steps back.

SW *raises C's r h, salutes.*	WM. I present to you Mr *Given Names Second*, a Candidate properly prepared to be made a Freemason.
WM	Bro. SW. *(salute)* Your presentation shall be attended to in due time. Meanwhile, you will instruct our Bro. JD to escort Mr *Second* from the lodge for a while.
SW	Bro. JD *(salute)* it is the Master's command that you escort Mr *Second* from the lodge for a while. *(JD escorts Second out.)*

T. Knocks of the Can. having prepared Mr Third

IG *salute*	Bro. JW. There is a report.
JW *salute*	WM. There is a report.
WM	Bro. JW. Enquire who wants admission.
JW *cuts S sit*	Bro. IG. See who seeks admission.

IG cuts S. Goes to the door and opens it to ask questions of the T.

IG *to T.*	Whom have you there?

T	Mr *Given Names Third*, a poor candidate in a state of d who has been well and worthily recommended, regularly proposed and approved in open Lodge, now comes of his own free will and accord, properly prepared and humbly soliciting to be admitted to the m and p of Ancient Freemasonry.
IG	How does he hope to obtain those privileges?
T	By the help of God, being free and of good report.

IG checks that the C is properly prepared. If he is, he proceeds:

IG	Wait, while I report to the WM.
IG *locks door, goes p'ment, salute.*	WM. Mr *Given Names Third*, a poor candidate in a state of d who has been well and worthily recommended, regularly proposed and approved in open Lodge, now comes of his own free will and accord, properly prepared and humbly soliciting to be admitted to the m and p of Ancient Freemasonry.
Guest GO 2 *from beside WM pedestal*	How does he hope to obtain those privileges?
IG	By the help of God, being free and of good report.
Guest GO 2	The tongue of good report has already been heard in his favour. Do you, Bro. IG, vouch that he is properly prepared?
IG	I do.
Guest GO 2	Admit him in due form. *(WM knocks)* Brother Ds.

IG cuts S, opens door when Ds are ready. Ds place kneeling stool on edge of p'ment. Go to door and take C, JD on C's right. IG applies p.

IG *to C*	Do you feel anything?
C prompt JD.	Yes.

Ds guide C to kneeling stool. IG raises p above C's head.

Guest GO 2	Mr *Third*, as no person can be made a Freemason unless he is free and of mature age, I demand are you free and of the full age of twenty one years?
C *prompt JD*	I am.

Guest GO 2	Then you will kneel while the blessing of heaven is invoked in aid of our proceedings.

Ds assist C to kneel. Place his r h on his l b, t d. Raise wands in arch over C. Stand to order, S of R. WM Gavels. Brethren S of R.

Chaplain	Vouchsafe Thine aid, Almighty Father, Supreme Governor of the Universe, to our present convention and grant that this candidate for Freemasonry may so dedicate and devote his life to Thy service as to become a true and faithful Brother amongst us. Endue him with a competency of Thy divine wisdom so that, assisted by the secrets of our Masonic art, he may be the better enabled to unfold the beauties of true Godliness, to the honour and glory of Thy holy name.
Brethren	So mote it be.
Guest GO 2	Mr *Third*, in all cases of difficulty and danger, in whom do you put your trust?
C *prompt JD*	In God.
Guest GO 2	Right glad am I to find your faith so well founded; relying on such sure support, you may safely rise and follow your leader with a firm but humble confidence, for where the name of God *(All drop S)* is invoked, we trust no danger will ensue. *(C stands. SD removes kneeling stool. Brethren sit.)*
WM *Gavel*	
Guest GO 2	Brethren in the N, E, S and W, take notice that Mr *Given Names Third* is about to pass in view before you to show that he is a Candidate properly prepared to be made a Freemason. *(sits)*
JD	Step off with the left foot.

Grips C with his l hand behind the C's right forearm, guides C past WM (no salute), to JW pedestal. With the C's r h, strikes the JW three times on the r s. SD follows to his seat.

JW *to JD*.	Whom have you there?

JD *salute*	Mr *Given Names Third*, a poor candidate in a state of d who has been well and worthily recommended, regularly proposed and approved in open Lodge, now comes of his own free will and accord, properly prepared and humbly soliciting to be admitted to the m and p of Ancient Freemasonry.
JW	How does he hope to obtain those privileges?
JD	By the help of God, *(cuts S)* being free and of good report.
JW *stand*	(*grasps C's r h in both of his*) Enter, free and of good report. *(Sits.)*

JD *waits until JW sits. Moves C back to pavement, then to right of SW. With the C's r h, strikes the SW three times on the r s.*

SW *to JD.*	Whom have you there?
JD *salute*	Mr *Given Names Third*, a poor candidate in a state of d who has been well and worthily recommended, regularly proposed and approved in open Lodge, now comes of his own free will and accord, properly prepared and humbly soliciting to be admitted to the m and p of Ancient Freemasonry.
SW	How does he hope to obtain those privileges?
JD	By the help of God, *(cuts S)* being free and of good report.
SW *stand*	(*grasps C's r h in both his*) Enter, free and of good report. (*Remains standing*.)

JD *guides C to the NW corner. Turns C so that SW can take C's r h. Squares C to face WM. Lets go of C and steps back.*

SW *raises C's rh, salute*	WM. I present to you Mr *Given Names Third*, a Candidate properly prepared to be made a Freemason.

Section TWO — Preparation for Obligation

WM	Bro. SW. *(salute)* Your presentation shall be attended to. To that end, you will instruct our Bro. Ds to return Mr *First* and Mr *Second* to the lodge.
	I will then address a few questions to the candidates which I trust they will answer with candour.

SW	Bro. Deacons, it is the Master's command that you return Mr *First* and Mr *Second* to the lodge. *(SD and D3 escort Mr First and Mr Second back into the lodge. JD passes Mr Third to D3 and takes command of Mr First. Line up N-S in front of SW.)*
SW *salute*	WM. I present to you Mr *First*, Mr *Second* and Mr *Third*, all candidates properly prepared to be made Freemasons.
WM	Mr *First* do you seriously declare on your honour that, unbiased by the improper solicitation of friends against your own inclination and uninfluenced by mercenary or other unworthy motives, you freely and voluntarily offer yourself a Candidate for the mysteries and privileges of Ancient Freemasonry?
C *prompt JD*	I do.
Guest GO 1	Mr Second and Mr Third, do you likewise so declare?
Cs	I do.
WM	Mr *Second*, do you likewise pledge yourself that you are prompted to solicit those privileges by a favourable opinion preconceived of the institution, a general desire for knowledge and a sincere wish to render yourself more extensively serviceable to your fellow creatures?
C *prompt JD*	I do.
Guest GO 2	Mr First and Mr Third, do you likewise so pledge yourself?
Cs	I do.
WM	Mr *Third*, do you further seriously declare on your honour that, avoiding fear on the one hand and rashness on the other, you will steadily persevere through the ceremony of your initiation and, if admitted, will ever afterwards act and abide by the ancient usages and established customs of the order?
C *prompt JD*	I do.
Guest GO 1	Mr First and Mr Second, do you likewise so declare?
Cs	I do.

WM	Bro. SW. *(salute.)* Direct that the candidates be instructed to advance to the E in due form.
SW *cuts S.*	Bro. Deacons. *(salute)* It is the WM's command that you instruct the candidates to advance to the E in due form.

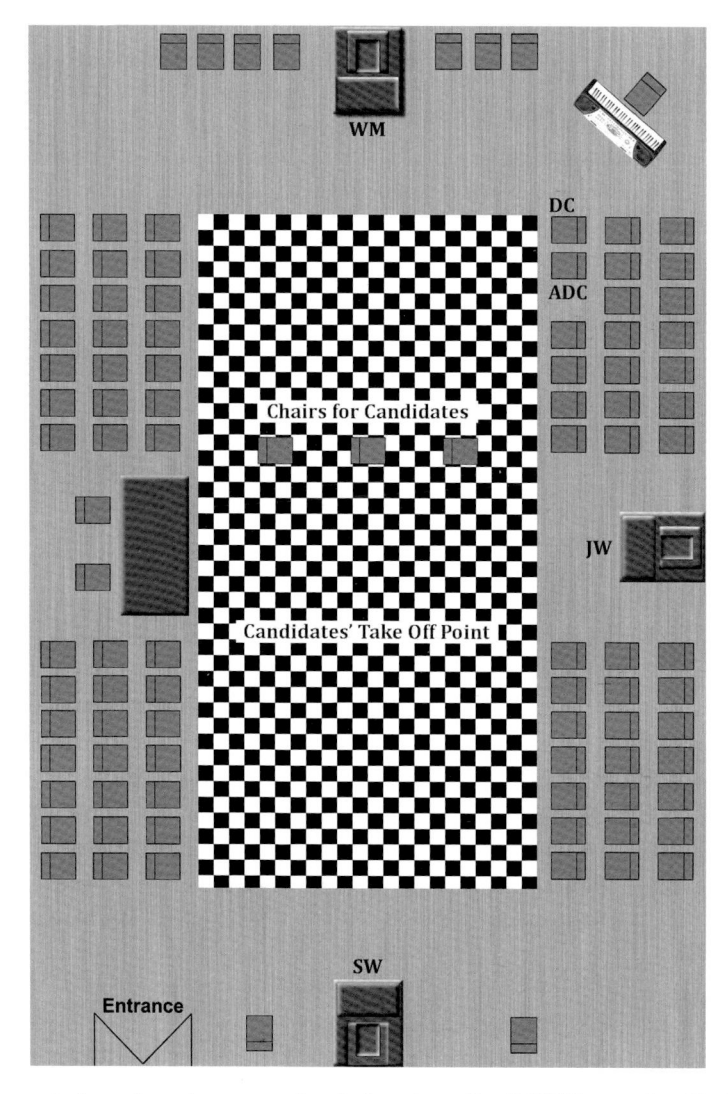

Three chairs placed across the lodge just E of JW/Sec axis. Cushion Bearers parade to each chair facing S, VSL and S&C on cushion and pr of cs behind. Cs brought to take off point, three steps from chairs. One C at a time is instructed to advance so they arrive in line at chairs.

WM	Mr *First*, Mr. *Second* and Mr *Third*, it is my duty to inform you that Masonry is free and requires a perfect freedom of inclination in every Candidate for its mysteries. It is founded on the purest principles of piety and virtue. It possesses many great and invaluable privileges and in order to secure those privileges to worthy men, and we trust to worthy men alone, vows of fidelity are required but let me assure you that in those vows there is nothing incompatible with your civil, moral or religious duties. Are you therefore willing to take a G and S O, founded on the principles I have stated, to keep inviolate the secrets and mysteries of the Order?
WM	Mr *First*?
First *prompt* JD	I am.
WM	Mr *Second*?
Second *prompt SD*	I am.
WM	Mr *Third* ?
Third *prompt* D3	I am

Section THREE — Obligations

The three brethren who will obligate the candidates step forward to face the candidates and obligate them one at a time. Ds raise wands over the candidate being obligated. Mr First and Second are invited to stand during other obligations if posture is uncomfortable but kneel again after Mr Third's obligation.

Obligator 1   Leads Mr *First* through the obligation.

Ob 1 removes cs and steps back. C remains kneeling.

Obligator 2   Leads Mr *Second* through the obligation.

Ob 2 removes cs and steps back. C remains kneeling.

Obligator 3   Leads Mr *Third* through the obligation.

Ob 3 removes cs. C remains kneeling. D's drop wands. Obligators 1 and 2 step forward in line with Obligator 3. All Candidates kneel again if they have stood for comfort.

WM *Ob's hand on C's, press VSL*	Mr *First*, as what you have repeated may be considered only a serious promise, as a pledge of fidelity and to render it a G and S O, you will seal it with your lips on this book, which is the VSL. *(Does so. JD assists)*
WM *Ob's hand on C's, press VSL*	Mr *Second* as what you have repeated may be considered only a serious promise, as a pledge of fidelity and to render it a G and S O, you will seal it with your lips on this book, which is the VSL. *(Does so. SD assists)*
WM *Ob's hand on C's, press VSL*	Mr *Third* as what you have repeated may be considered only a serious promise, as a pledge of fidelity and to render it a G and S O, you will seal it with your lips on this book, which is the VSL. *(Does so. D3 assists)*
WM	Having been kept for a considerable time in a state of d, what in your present condition is the predominant wish of your heart?
JD	Answer all together, L. *(Cs do so)*
WM	Let that blessing be restored to the candidates.

Ds undo bows but hold the strings so b remains in place. When ready, give nod to WM. When all three ready, WM raises gavel (three count) swings the gavel to the left (1) to the right (2) and then down with blow to the pedestal (3). On (3), the D's release b and brethren give one clap. Ds gently press C's heads forward so their eyes are directed at the VSL.

WM	Having been restored to the blessing of material L, I will now direct your attention to what we consider the three great, though emblematical Ls in Freemasonry. *(Obs indicate.)* They are the V of the SL, the S, and the Cs. The S Ws are to govern our faith, the S to regulate our actions and the Cs to keep us in due bounds with all mankind, particularly our brethren in Freemasonry.
Ob 1 *Bro. First*	Rise duly obligated *(emph)* **Brother** among Masons.
Ob 2 *Bro. Second*	Rise duly obligated *(emph)* **Brother** among Masons.
Ob 3 *Bro. Third*	Rise duly obligated *(emph)* **Brother** among Masons.

Cushion Bearers return to seats. Chairs removed. Obligators sit. Guest GO 1 and 2 step forward. GO 1 to Sec table, GO 2 to SW pedestal

Guest GO 1	You are now enabled to discover the three Ls in Freemasonry which are situated in the E, S and W and are meant to represent the Sun (*indicates JW*), the Moon (*indicates SW*) and the M of the Lodge (*indicates WM*) The Sun to rule the day; the Moon to govern the night and the M to rule and direct his Lodge. (*Pause for emphasis*) **Brethren**. (*Cue for IG*) by your meek and candid behaviour this evening, you have symbolically escaped two great dangers; those of s and s.

IG with P held across l forearm in s, h facing outwards, moves to WM pedestal, arrives at GO, "For on your entrance to the Lodge, this P."

Guest GO 1	For on your entrance to the Lodge, this P (*etc.*) was presented to your n l b (*points towards each C in turn — without moving*) to imply that had you rashly attempted to rush forward, you would have been an accessory to your d by s for the Brother who held it would have remained firm (*etc.*) and done his duty.

IG returns to seat. Ds lifts c t over C's head. JD offers c t to GO 2.

Guest GO 2	There was likewise this c t with a r n about your n, (*etc.*) to symbolise that any attempt at retreat would have proved equally (*etc.*) fatal. (*Gives c t to D.*)
Guest GO 2	But traditionally there was a third danger which would have awaited you until your latest hour, namely a physical penalty at one time associated with the O of a Freemason. It was that of having *etc.* had you improperly disclosed the secrets of Freemasonry. The inclusion of such a penalty is unnecessary for the obligation you have taken this evening is binding upon you for as long as you shall live. *GOs sit.*

Section FOUR — communication of secrets

WM	Having taken the G and SO of an EA Freemason, I am now permitted to inform you that there are several degrees in Freemasonry with peculiar secrets restricted to each. These, however, are not communicated indiscriminately but are conferred upon candidates according to merit and ability.

WM (cont.)	I shall therefore proceed to entrust you with the secrets of this degree, or those marks by which we are known to each other and distinguished from the rest of the world, but must premise for your general information that all Ss, Ls and Ps are true and proper Ss by which to know a Freemason.

Ds assists C to copy the WM's instructions, following suit themselves.

WM	You will therefore stand perfectly erect, your feet in the form of a s, your body thus being considered an emblem of your mind and your feet of the rectitude of your actions. You will now take a s s towards me towards me with your l f, placing the h of the r into its h. *(Points)* That, my brethren, is the f r s in Freemasonry and it is in that position that the secrets of the degree are communicated. They consist of a S, T and W. *(Stands)* Please copy me. The S is given *(etc.)* This, you will perceive, alludes to the symbolic p of the degree which implied that as a man of honour, an EA Freemason would rather have had etc. than improperly disclose the secrets of Freemasonry. *(sits)*

Three Obligators step forward to assist with demonstration of the g.

WM	The G or T is given *(etc.)* This G, when mutually given and received, serves to distinguish a brother by night as well as by day. It also demands a word; a word highly prized among Freemasons as a safeguard to their privileges. Too much caution, therefore, cannot be observed in communicating it. It should **never** *(stresses this word)* be given at length as you are about to receive it but always by letters or syllables. To enable you to do which, I will tell you the word. It is ….
JD	Answer all together, ...
WM	Spells out W.
JD	Answer all together, *(spells out W and C's repeat)* ....

Examination sequence one

WM	As in the course of the ceremony you will be called upon for this word, our Brother Ds will now dictate the answers you are to give.

Ob 1 *to First*	What is this?
First *prompt JD*	The G or T of an EA Freemason.
Ob 1	What does this G demand?
First *prompt JD*	A W.
Ob 1	Give me that W.

JD *grasps C's arm firmly.*

First *prompt JD*	/ *indicates pauses to allow Cs to repeat*. At my initiation / I was taught to be cautious / but I will l / or h it with you.
Ob 1	H it and begin.

First, prompt JD, gives first s, Ob 1 second and First the w.

Sequence two

Ob 2 *to Second*	What is this?
Second *prompt SD*	The G or T of an EA Freemason.
Ob 2	What does this G demand?
Second *prompt SD*	A W.
Ob 2	Give me that W.

SD *Grasps C's arm firmly.*

Second *prompt SD*	/ *indicates pauses to allow Cs to repeat*. At my initiation / I was taught to be cautious / but I will l / or h it with you.
Ob 2	L it and begin.

Second, prompt JD, gives first l, Ob 2 second etc.

Sequence three

Ob 3 to Third	What is this?
Third *prompt D3*	The G or T of an EA Freemason.
Ob 3	What does this G demand?

166

Third *prompt* D3	A W.
Ob 3	Give me that W.

D grasps C's arm firmly.

Third *prompt* D3	/ *here indicate pauses to allow C to repeat.* At my initiation / I was taught to be cautious / but I will l / or h it with you.
Ob 3	H it and begin.

Third, prompt D3, gives first s, Ob 3 second and Third the w.

WM	This w is derived from the l h p that stood at the p e of K S T, so named after … a G G of D, a P and R in I. The import of the W is ….

Pass one at a time

Ob 1 *to First*	Pass ...
Ob 2 *to Second*	Pass ...
Ob 3 *to Third*	Pass ... *Obligators return to their seats.*

Section FIVE — presentations

Candidates are presented to JW and SW. Each time, First taken by JD to Warden, Second by SD to DC standing in front of pedestal, Third by D3 to IPM, standing outside DC. IPM & DC say, "Pass …" in turn after W has said it. After JW exam, DC and IPM immediately take position for SW exam.

JD	*(At JW pedestal)* Bro. JW, *(salute)* I present to you Brothers *First, Second* and *Third* on their initiation.
JW	I will thank Brothers *First, Second* and *Third* to advance to me as an EA Freemason, showing the S. *(JD instructs Cs to step and S then cut.*
JW	Have you anything to communicate?
JD/Cs	Answer all together, I have. *(JW Stands and extends his hand to the Can. JD Places C's h in the correct manner. Repeated by DC and IPM with their Cs.)*
JW	What is this?
JD/Cs	Answer all together, the G or T of an EA Freemason.

JW	What does this G demand?
JD/Cs	Answer all together, a W.
JW	Give me that W. *(JD Grasps C's arm firmly.)*
JD/Cs	*/ indicates pauses to allow Cs to repeat.* Answer all together, at my initiation / I was taught to be cautious / but I will l / or h it with you.
JW	H it and begin.
JD/Cs	Answer all together ...

Cans, prompted by JD, give first s, the JW the second and Cs the W.

Individually passed

JW to First   Pass ...

DC to Second   Pass ...

IPM to Third   Pass ...

DC and IPM take post N of SW pedestal, facing S. Ds wait until JW sits, then guide Cs to SW pedestal.

JD	Bro. SW, *(salute)* I present to you Brothers *First*, *Second* and *Third* on their initiation.
SW	I will thank Brothers *First*, *Second* and *Third* to advance to me as an EA Freemason (*JD instructs Cs.*)
SW	*(Points.)* What is that?
JD/Cs	Answer all together, the first r s in Freemasonry.
SW	Do you bring anything with you?
JD/Cs	Answer all together, I do. *(Shows the S.)*
SW	What is that?
JD/Cs	Answer all together, the S of an EA Freemason.
SW	To what does it allude?
JD/Cs	*/ indicates pauses to allow Cs to repeat.* Answer all together, to the symbolic p of the degree / which implied that / as a man of honour / an EA Freemason / would rather have had (*etc.*) than improperly disclose / the secrets of Freemasonry.
SW	Have you anything to communicate?

168

JD/Cs	Answer all together, I have. *(SW stands. Cs, guided by Ds, give the G.)*
SW	What is this?
JD/Cs	Answer all together, the G or T of an EA Freemason.
SW	What does this g demand?
JD/Cs	Answer all together, a W.
SW	Give me that W.
JD / Cs	*/ indicates pauses to allow Cs to repeat.* Answer all together, at my initiation / I was taught to be cautious / but I will l / or h it with you.
SW	H it and begin.
JD	Answer all together ...

Cs, prompted by Ds, give first s, the SW the second and the Cs the W.

SW	Whence is this W derived?
JD / Cs	*/ indicates pauses to allow Cs to repeat.* Answer all together, from the l h p / that stood at the p e / of KST, / so named after ..., / a GG of D, / a P and R in I.
SW	The import of the W?
JD/Cs	Answer all together, in s.

Individually passed

SW to First	Pass ...
DC to Second	Pass ...
IPM to Third	Pass ...

DC returns to collect aprons. IPM returns to seat. SW remains standing. JD guides First so that his r h can be grasped by SW. SD guides Second so his rh is on First's shoulder. D3 guides Third so his rh is on Second's shoulder. All Ds stand behind. The line should be at an angle from pedestal, roughly towards SE.

SW	*(Lifts First's hand.)* WM. I present to you Brothers *First*, *Second* and *Third* on their initiation for some mark of your favour.
WM	Bro. SW. I delegate you to invest our Brothers with the distinguishing badge *(gestures to aprons on cushion)* of an EA Freemason. Bros PM1 and PM2, please assist.

PM1 and PM2 walk forward to face Second and Third. DC offers aprons to SW, PM1 and PM2 and then steps well back. Aprons put on. SW, PM1 and PM2 hold corner of aprons.

SW	Brothers *First, Second* and *Third* , by command of the WM, I invest you with the distinguishing badge of an EA Freemason.

PM1	It is more ancient than the Golden Fleece or Roman Eagle, more honourable than the Star, Garter or any order in existence.

PM2	It is the badge of innocence and the bond of friendship and we strongly exhort you ever to wear and consider it as such.

SW	I further inform you that if you never disgrace that *(raises arm as signal)* badge *(strikes apron, brethren give one clap)*, it will never disgrace you.

SW sits. PM2 & 2 sit. PM3 steps to C of lodge. DC takes cushion back.

PM3	Brethren, you are never to put on that badge should you be about to enter a Lodge wherein there is a Brother with whom you are at variance or against whom you entertain feelings of animosity. In such a case, it is expected that you will invite him to withdraw in order to settle your differences amicably which if happily effected, you may clothe, enter the Lodge and work with that love and harmony which should at all times characterise Freemasons. But if, unfortunately, your differences are of such a nature as not to be so easily adjusted it were better that one or both of you retire than that the harmony of the Lodge be disturbed by your presence. *(Salutes WM and returns to his seat.)*

Ds regain Cs. Step to pavement, JD to S, SD to centre and D3 N, face E

WM	Bro. Deacons. *(Ds salute.)* Place our Brothers in the NE part of the Lodge.

Ds — in turn JD first — instruct Cs to step off with lf and guide them to the NE corner in a line facing S.

JD	L f across the Lodge, r f down the Lodge.

IPM	*(Stands and steps forward onto pavement.)* It is customary at the erection of all stately and superb edifices to lay the first or foundation stone in the NE corner of the intended building. You being newly admitted into Freemasonry are placed in the NE *(indicate with hand)* part of the Lodge, figuratively to represent that stone and on the foundation laid this evening may you raise a superstructure, perfect in its parts and honourable to the builder.
	You now stand to all appearance a just and upright EA Freemason and I give it to you in terms of strong recommendation ever to continue and act as such. Indeed, I will immediately proceed to put your principles in some measure to the test by calling upon you to exercise that virtue which may justly be denominated the distinguishing characteristic of a Freemason's heart. I mean charity. I need not here dilate upon its excellencies. Doubtless it has often been felt and practised by you. Suffice to say it hath the approbation of heaven and earth and like its sister, mercy, blesses him who gives as well as him who receives.
	In a society so widely extended as that of Freemasonry, whose branches are spread over the four quarters of the globe, it cannot be denied that we have many members of rank and opulence. Neither can it be concealed that, among the thousands ranged under its banner, there are some who from circumstances of unforeseen calamity and misfortune are reduced to the lowest ebb of poverty and distress. On their behalf, it is our usual custom to awaken the feelings of every newly made Brother by making such an appeal to his charity as his circumstances in life may fairly warrant. Whatever, therefore, you feel disposed to give will be thankfully received and faithfully applied.
'Voice from crowd'1	Bro. *First*, have you anything to give in the cause of charity? (*D3 proffers collection box.*)
First *unprompted*	No – *or words to that effect.*

'Voice from crowd' 2	Bro. Second, have you anything to give in the cause of charity? (*D3 proffers collection box.*)
Second *unprompted*	No – *or words to that effect.*
'Voice from crowd' 3	Bro. Third, have you anything to give in the cause of charity? (*D3 proffers collection box.*)
Third *unprompted*	No – *or words to that effect.* (*D3 returns to place.*)
IPM	Were you, each one of you, divested of m and ms previous to entering the Lodge?
Cs *unprompted.*	Yes – *or words to that effect.*
IPM	Otherwise would all of you have given freely?
Cs *unprompted.*	Yes – *or words to that effect.*
IPM	(*Salute*) WM, our brethren express their willingness but plead inability, having been divested of all m and m s previous to entering the Lodge. Otherwise they would all have given freely. (*sits*)
WM	Brethren, I congratulate you on the honourable sentiments by which you are actuated; likewise on the inability which in the present instance precludes you from gratifying them.
	Believe me, my Brothers, this trial was not made with a view to sport with your feelings. Far be from us any such intention. It was made for three especial reasons: first, as I have already premised, to put your principles to the test; secondly, to evince to the brethren that you had neither m nor m s about you for if you had the ceremony of your initiation thus far must have been repeated; and thirdly as a warning to your heart, that should you at any time meet a friend or Brother in distressed circumstances who might solicit your assistance, you will remember the peculiar moment you were received into Freemasonry p and p and cheerfully embrace the opportunity of practising that virtue you now profess to admire.

WM	*(gavel)* Brethren, the WTs of an Entered Apprentice Freemason will this evening be given by Bro. MM.

Cs remain in a line. Explanation given by MM from centre of lodge. ADC holds WTs on cushion. MM salutes WM and returns to seat. MM2 collects warrant from WM and assists Treasurer who comes out to face Cs, as does Secretary after him.

Treasurer	As during the course of the evening you will be called upon for certain fees for your initiation, it is but right that you know by what authority we act. *(shows warrant)* This is our charter or warrant of constitution from the Grand Lodge of England which is available for your inspection at this or any subsequent Lodge meeting.

Shows warrant, returns it to MM2 who returns it to WM.

Secretary	This is the Book of Constitutions and this our By-Laws, both of which I recommend to your serious perusal, as by the one *(gives each B of C)* you may learn the duties you owe to the Craft in general and by the other *(gives By-laws)* to this Lodge in particular. Other instructive documentation will be given to you after the meeting, including the answers you must give to certain questions to qualify you for the ceremony of passing. *(Sits) (D3 leads Cs to face WM line across at SW level.)*
WM	You are now at liberty to retire in order to restore your personal comforts and on your return to the Lodge, I shall direct your attention to an Ancient Charge founded on the excellencies of the Institution and the qualifications of its members.

D3 leads line to NW. JD calls for salutes. JD leads exit by turning 180 degrees and walking towards door. All follow, turning at same point. Call off. Tea. Call on.

One knock. IG stands forward and salutes.

IG	Bro. SW, there is a report.

SW looks at WM who nods. SW gives one knock. IG goes to door.

IG	Whom have you there?
T	The three candidates on their return.

IG	Wait while I report to the WM. *(Closes door and steps to the pavement)*
IG *salute*	WM, the candidates on their return.
WM	Admit them, Bro. IG. *(knocks)* Bro. Ds.

Ds bring Cans into the lodge and line them up in the W.

JD	Salute the WM previous to entering the lodge. *(do so.)*
WM *gavel*	Brethren, Bro. Guest GO 3 now has a pleasing duty to perform.

Ds bring Cans to SW-Sec axis. DC steps forward with cushion bearing three pairs of gloves. Guest GO 3 steps forward, salutes the WM and presents gloves to each candidate in a short ceremony. GO 3 salutes and returns to his seat. DC returns to seat.

GO3　　In France, Germany and other countries of Europe, it is the custom to present the newly-initiated candidate not only, as we do, with a white leather apron, but also with two pairs of white kid gloves; one a man's pair for himself, and the other a woman's. These are to be presented by him in turn to his wife, his betrothed, or otherwise to the lady whom he most esteems.

There is in this, as there is in everything else which pertains to Freemasonry, a symbolism. The gloves given to the candidate for himself are intended to teach him that the acts of a Mason should be as pure and spotless as the gloves now given to him.

There are numerous references in sacred and profane writers to this symbolism. The washing of the hands has the outward sign of an internal purification. Hence the Psalmist says,

I will wash my hands in innocence, and I will encompass thine altar.

In the Christian church of the middle ages, gloves were always worn by bishops or priests during the performance of ecclesiastical functions. They were made of linen, and were white denoting chastity and purity. Gloved, the hands were kept clean and free from all impurity.

	(This example drawn from the writing of Albert Mackay but GO3 should be free to create his own description.)
WM *gavel*	Thankyou Bro. GO3. Brethren, the charge after initiation will be given by Bro. PM5.

DC steps forward and guides PM5 to the centre of lodge. Salutes the WM, delivers charge. Salutes again. DC escorts him to his seat.

Mentor	*(Salute)* Brother *First*, I have asked Bro. PM6 to act as your personal guide and mentor. He will explain and help you to understand the recent ceremony and also the ceremonies to follow. He will also explain the customs and traditions of our ancient institution. *(PM6 steps forward and shakes hands.)* Brother *Second*, Bro. PM7 will act as your personal guide and mentor *(handshake)* and Brother *Third*, PM8 will be your mentor. *(handshake. Mentors sit.)*
Chaplain	To mark this occasion, the members of the Lodge of Instruction have asked me, as Chaplain, to present each of you with the VSL on which you took your obligation. I hope that you will treasure it as a memento of this wonderful occasion. Bro. *First (gives VSL)*. Bro. *Second (gives VSL)*. Bro. *Third (gives VSL)*. *(Salutes WM and sits.)*
WM	Brother *First*, I congratulate you on your becoming a member of our ancient and honourable Institution. *(Taken forward to shake hands, stepping back afterwards.)* Brother *Second*, I congratulate you on your becoming a member of our ancient and honourable Institution. *(Ditto.)* Brother *Third*, I congratulate you also on your becoming a member of our ancient and honourable Institution. *(Ditto) (To all)* I take great pleasure in welcoming you to this lodge and look forward to enjoying your Masonic progress. Bro. Deacons, place our brethren in convenient seats in the lodge. *(Placed next to SD.)* *End*

Music for *Exposure!*

composed and arranged by Eric Stuckey. Bro. Eric's recording of the music for *Exposure!* can be downloaded free at
http://stlaurencelodge.org.uk/publications/entertainments/

House of the Rising Sun

Trad.
arranged for Violin & Viola
by Eric Stuckey

© 2000

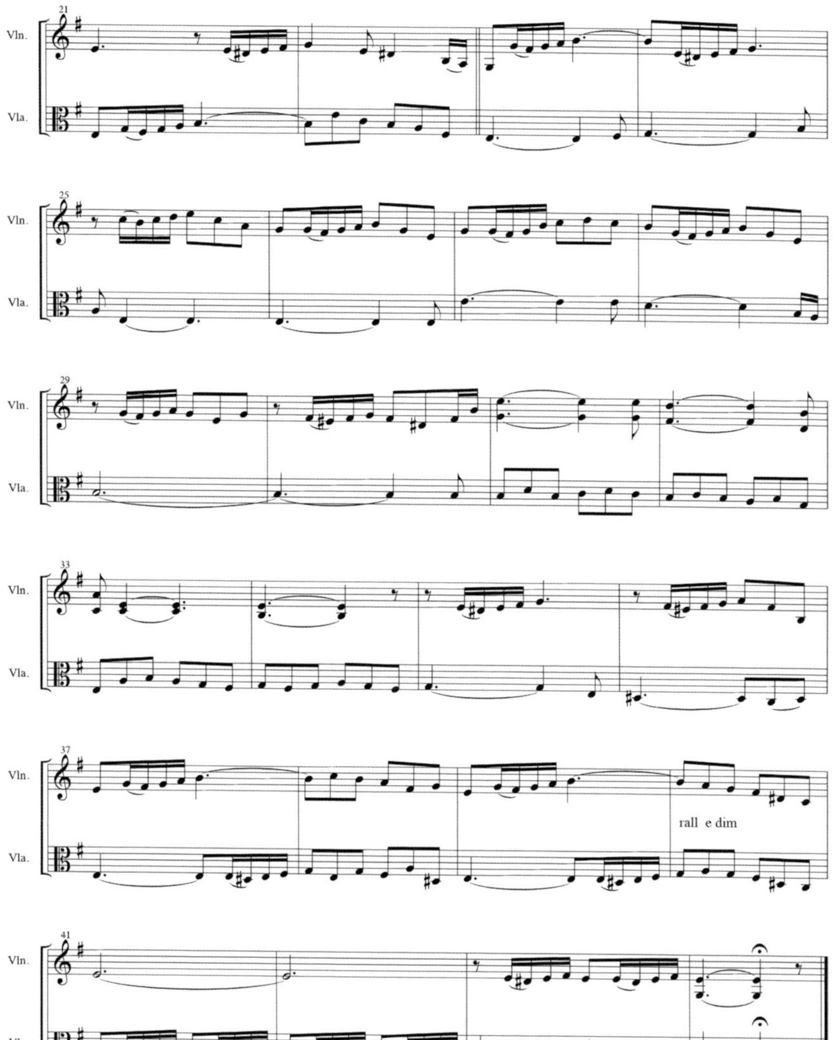
Vln.
Vla.
rall e dim

No 10 Duke Street

Original Music and Let us take the Road
from The Beggar's Opera

Written & arranged for Violin & Viola
"Based at 10 Duke St."

Eric Stuckey

178

STOP AT "Puppet Strings of the Craft"

"Step Forward"

The Modes of The Court

Arr. for Violin & Viola
by Eric Stuckey

From The Beggar's Opera
"Come back with us to 1730"

Traditional Irish Melody
Lilliburlero

Bro. Eric Stuckey — composer and arranger.

A Catch

Fill, fill your glasses round, and each man pledge his fellow

"29 Pages 6 Pence"

Dr. William Hayes 1708 - 1777

STOP AT SIGN FROM D.C.

Entered Apprentices Song

Arr. for Violin & Viola

Eric Stuckey

© 1998

No longer apprentices. Two brethren who celebrate 60 years as Freemasons, seen with our current Assistant Provincial Grand Master.

Opening Ode

arr for Violin & Viola
by Eric Stuckey

God only Great & Wise & Strong

Dr. Mainzer

Bro. Guy, a Past Master

The Gamesters & Lawyers
from The Beggar's Opera

arr. for Violin & Viola by Eric Stuckey

Melody taken from Musick's Hand-maid

STOP when Ready

So J... is the real EA Word   and B... is really the FC word

© 1998

Youth's the Season

COTILLON
From The Beggar's Opera

arr. for Violin & Viola
by Eric Stuckey

French Dance Tune from
Lesage's "Télémaque"

arrangement © 1998

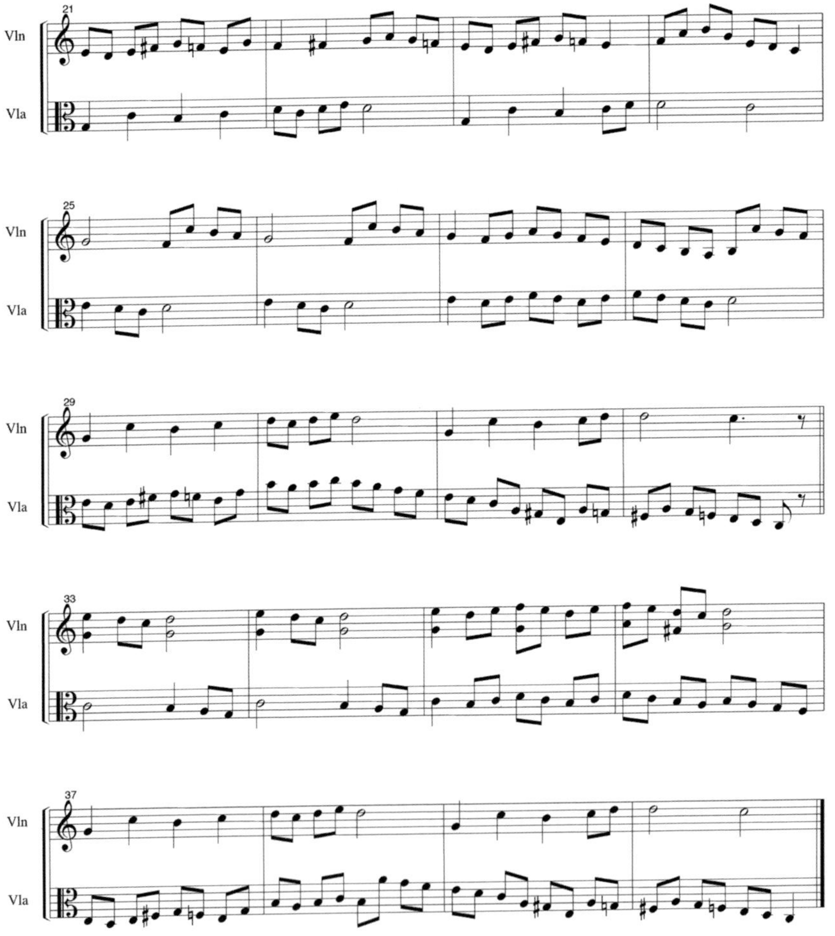
21
Vln
Vla
25
Vln
Vla
29
Vln
Vla
33
Vln
Vla
37
Vln
Vla

Mason's Apron
English Folk Dance

2

Bro. Steve, jumping charitably.

Err from Godliness

Eric Stuckey

"err from Godliness" then Actor pushes other Actor from soap box

Dance à la Ronde

From the Beggar's Opera

arr. for Violin & Viola
by Eric Stuckey

John Gay

© 1998

The queue for a dance with the Lady President.

Works mentioned in the text

Versions of Lectures

The Lectures of the Three Degrees in Craft Masonry as demonstrated in the Emulation Lodge of Improvement, Lewis Masonic, third edition 2012
M.M. Taylor's Sections on Craft Freemasonry giving the questions and answers appertaining to each degree, Lewis Masonic 2008.

Other works

Beresiner, Yasha; *The Freemason's Handbook of Toasts, Speeches and Responses*, Lewis Masonic, 2009.
Carr, Harry; *The Freemason at Work*, Lewis Masonic, sixth edition, 1981.
Dyer, Colin; *William Preston and his work*, Lewis Masonic, 1987.
Foot, Sarah; *Æthelstan, The First King Of England*, Yale University Press, 2011
Haunch, T.O; *It is not in the power of any man ... A Study in Change*, Prestonian Lecture for 1972, re-published in *The Collected Prestonian Lectures*, Volume Two, 1961-1974, *Quatuor Coronati* Lodge, 1983.
Jones, Bernard E.; *Freemasons' Guide and Compendium*, Harrap, 1950.
Knoop, Douglas; Jones GP; Hamer, Douglas (eds), *The Early Masonic Catechisms*, second edition, *Quatuor Coronati* Lodge, 1975.
Knoop, Douglas; Jones GP; Hamer, Douglas (eds), *The Early Masonic Pamphlets*, Manchester University Press 1945, *Quatuor Coronati* Lodge, 1978.
Knight, Stephen; *The Brotherhood*, Granada Books, 1983 reprinted by Panther Books, 1985.
McLeod, Wallace; *The Old Charges*, Prestonian Lecture for 1986, re-published in *The Collected Prestonian Lectures*, Volume Three, 1975-1987, Lewis Masonic, 1988.
Neville, Mike; *Sacred Secrets*, The History Press, 2012.
Putnam, Robert B; *Bowling Alone: the collapse and revival of American community*, Touchstone Books, 2001.
Prichard, Samuel; *Masonry Dissected* in *The Early Masonic Catechisms*, Douglas Knoop, GP Jones & Douglas Hamer, second edition ed. Harry Carr, *Quatuor Coronati* Lodge, 1975.
Ripperologist magazine, June 2002.
Vibert, Lionel; *The Development of the Trigradal System*, Prestonian Lecture for 1925, re-published in *The Collected Prestonian Lectures*, Volume One, 1925-1960, Lewis Masonic, 1984.
West, David; *The Goat, the Devil and the Freemason*, Hamilton House, 2013.

Additional photographs

Stephen Knight, photograph probably by Richard Whittington-Egan.
Seddon case, source unknown.
Hogarth, fourth in *Four Stages of Cruelty*, 1751, in public domain.
Aldworth Plaque, ShadowRAM, Wikimedia Commons.
Shriner, Rdikeman, Wikimedia Commons.
Mourning Rosettes, Lewis Masonic catalogue.

Other books by David West

The Goat, the Devil and the Freemason

'*Brilliantly researched, erudite and entertaining, a perfect counterpoint to all the pretentious rubbish about Freemasonry, a fascinating story that deserves to be read.*'

A magical history tour of goats and devils and how they became associated with Freemasonry.

(Cover design Lawrie Morrisson)

Employee Engagement and the failure of leadership

Written for *The Working Manager Ltd* on the occasion of his retirement from the company he created, the book summarises Dr West's views on the reality of employee engagement and the reasons why most companies fail to achieve it.

It is not something that the HR department can take care of while line management gets on with the job. It is the essence of leadership and the failure of engagement is the failure of leadership.

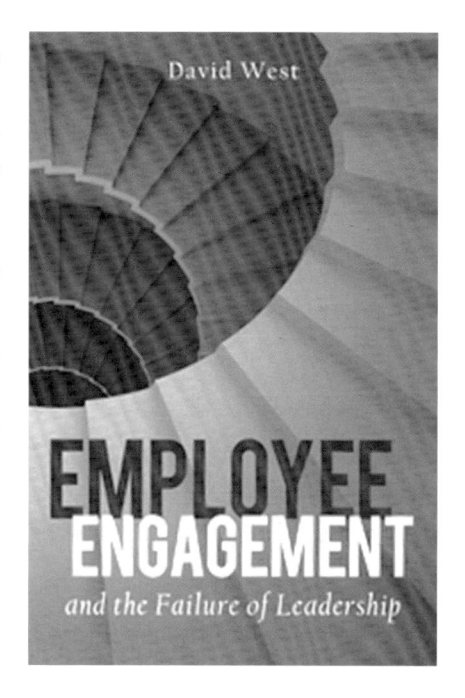

Dr David West

… gained his first degree in Philosophy from the University of Exeter and his Doctorate of and in Philosophy from the University of Leicester. He taught at Leicester University and at Acadia University in Canada. His business career included Ford and Xerox. He served on several committees on the future of work, was special adviser to a cabinet minister, and founded *The Working Manager Ltd*, creating the core content of its web based management education process. Dr West is a member of three lodges and four chapters in the English Constitution. He has served as Grand Registrar of the Masonic Province of Essex and is now Past Provincial Junior Grand Warden. This is his second Masonic book.

Lawrie Morrisson

… is a member of the Institution of Engineering and Technology. His career as an electrical engineer focused on building services, designing installations for various premises including schools, sheltered housing and public buildings. Prior to his retirement in 2009, he was Group Manager responsible for all electrical design and maintenance works for a local authority in East London. He has an appetite for IT and has become proficient in image manipulation and website design while undertaking professional studies in photography. Secretary of St Laurence Lodge No. 5511 and Past Provincial Assistant Grand Director of Ceremonies in the Masonic Province of Essex, he created and manages the lodge website. He is also a Royal Arch Mason.